Strong, Loving and Wise

Presiding in Liturgy

by Robert W. Hovda
Foreword by Godfrey Diekmann, O.S.B.

THE LITURGICAL PRESS
Collegeville, Minnesota

The Ministry Series published by The Liturgical Press:

The Ministry of Ushers
Gregory F. Smith, O.Carm.

The Ministry of Lectors
James A. Wallace, C.SS.R.

The Ministry of Servers
Michael Kwatera, O.S.B.

The Ministry of Communion
Michael Kwatera, O.S.B.

The Ministry of Believers
Emeric A. Lawrence, O.S.B.

The Ministry of Musicians
Edward J. McKenna

The Ministry of Liturgical Environment
Thomas G. Simons and James M. Fitzpatrick

The Ministry of the Cantor
James Hansen

The Liturgical Ministry of Deacons
Michael Kwatera, O.S.B.

The Ministry of Parents to Teenagers
Simeon J. Thole, O.S.B.

ISBN 0-918208-12-2 (First four printings); ISBN 0-8146-1253-9 (Fifth and sixth printings). Library of Congress Catalog Card Number 76-56474

Fourth printing, September 1980 by The Liturgical Conference. Fifth printing, April 1983 by The Liturgical Press (cover photo of fifth printing courtesy of the Public Information Office, St. John's Abbey, Collegeville, Minnesota). Sixth printing, September 1985 by The Liturgical Press (cover photo and design by Placid Stuckenschneider, O.S.B.). Other photos are from the film "Many Different Gifts" by Jim Furlong with the Nova Community of Northern Virginia.

Contents

Foreword

One of the standard exercises of priests' retreats in pre-Vatican II days was the so-called "dry mass": someone, usually the retreat master, went through the motions of celebrating the eucharist, meanwhile exhorting his listeners to correctness of rubrical performance. He reminded them that, since the mass effected its results *ex opere operato* and, above all, since Christ himself continued to be the chief celebrant and they only represented him, they must not allow any personal emotion or interpretation to find expression in their actions. There was to be nothing subjective. Their ideal was to remain "the faceless priest."

This seems to be a good instance of a frightfully wrong conclusion drawn from unexceptionable (if incomplete) premises.

The ordained minister is not a true "sacrament" of Christ, of him who delivered himself up for love of us, by acting as a nerveless automaton. And yet priests, in unquestioning obedience to rubrical directives, for centuries adopted the completely meaningless "cigar-box" stance in prayer at the altar; and the extension of hands, in imitation of Christ's extended arms on the cross embracing all humankind in compassionate love, became in the early days of the liturgical movement *prima facie* proof of a "liturgical extremist." How long ago those days now seem!

There is also, of course, another dimension of the presider himself being an integral component of the sacrament of the eucharist, one whose pastoral implications Father Hovda develops in this book with admirable persuasiveness. We used to talk about "the distribution of roles" in the eucharistic liturgy. But it obviously is not just a matter of the priest having to perform x-percent of the action, the ministers and choir y-percent, and the congregation the remaining z-percent.

The priest is not only "sacrament" of Christ, he is also—and above all in his praying of the great eucharistic prayer—"sacrament" of the entire people of God. And a sacrament both signifies and effects; or rather, as Thomas Aquinas reminds us, "by signifying it effects."

It is the presider's role to signify, to give visible expression to the faith and devotion of the congregation. And only by signifying well himself, and by his passionate concern that the prayers and rites at which he presides signify as they were meant to, does he fulfill his sacramental, priestly role of effecting: of being Christ's agent in deepening his people's faith, of inflaming their love. No one can take his place. All else is palliative. Genuine participation of the congregation in the liturgy depends to an almost frightening degree, not only on whether the presider "puts on" Christ, but also on whether he accepts his role of being the "sacrament" of his people.

To borrow the witty judgment of a church historian: the Donatists may have been wrong theologically, but they were pastorally, oh, so right.

It is an honor for me to contribute this brief foreword to Father Hovda's new and important work. I have long been an admirer of his bulletin, *Living Worship*, which I look forward to every month as I used to look forward with pleasant anticipation to the "Timely Tract" of Father Reinhold (H.A.R.) in *Worship*. It is pastoral liturgical writing of a consistently high calibre, based on sound theology. And so is this book.

—Godfrey Diekmann, O.S.B.

Introduction

"There will never come an end to the good that he has done." That inscription on a Grand Canyon overlook memorial to Ting Mather is one that expresses simply and without excess the effect of any person whose deed enables an important and good experience for another person or for many people. It is therefore an appropriate tribute to any presider in a liturgical assembly who functions well in that role Sunday after Sunday and year after year.

Believers gather nowhere else in such numbers, with such regularity and for so profound a purpose. To be in a position to touch them on sensitive and vulnerable levels of their beings—levels possibly though not necessarily exposed in their public ritual action—is to be terribly vulnerable oneself. It invites, even demands, a strong vocational commitment to work, a loving compassion for people, and a wise acceptance of one's limits and God's reign.

The fact that this manual appears subsequently to The Liturgical Conference's guidebooks for liturgy committees, readers, musicians, and a combined one for acolytes, ministers of communion, ushers and other occasional ministers is not an indication of low priority for its subject. The men and women who preside at services of Christian public worship in the United States and Canada on Saturday evenings and Sundays are in at least some contact with an astonishingly large percentage of church members.

While it is true that ecclesial renewal depends, first of all, on the local congregation's awakening to and involvement in the meaning of baptism-confirmation-eucharist, on the whole church's experience of initiation and commitment, there is no single office of servanthood within that community more important as a potential enabler and sustainer of renewal than the office of the one who presides in liturgy.

This manual can aspire to serve the broad spectrum of those persons who preside in public rites because it contains very little that is original. It is a collection of the ideas and experiences of many pastoral practitioners and many congregations. While the author accepts responsibility for its statements, he owes them to a lifetime of ecclesial experience and to a host of teachers, priests, friends and writers, as well as to the membership, staff and board of directors of The Liturgical Conference.

The Liturgical Conference publishes this book with theological schools and seminaries in mind, bishops, priests, pastors, deacons, any others who regularly preside in public worship, and those responsible for continuing education programs for clergy. Its intent is to serve both those who preside in liturgy and those who are training for offices which will involve such presiding. Since 1940 The Liturgical Conference has been a voluntary membership association—at first only of Catholics in communion with the Roman church but more recently including many other Christians— persons concerned with the liturgical life and vitality of the churches. Membership is chiefly in the United States and Canada. Its office, workshops, publications, Liturgical Weeks and other meetings embrace the gamut of human prayer and ritual needs and expressions, with particular emphasis on the specific ecclesial-liturgical dimension under discussion here.

The problems confronted in this guidebook are ecumenical, so our intent is ecumenical, an approach facilitated by The Liturgical Conference's interconfessional, international and independent character. While the author's adult experience is in the liturgical traditions of the Roman rite, this is no handicap to a broader sharing, as Christians of sacramental traditions increasingly appreciate the biblical word as integral to ritual action and those of traditions which have emphasized the word show a revived interest in the fullness of symbol, sacrament and liturgy.

The term "presider" is used throughout, as much as possible without masculine or feminine pronouns. "Presiding" and "presider" are more accurate than the common "celebrating" and "celebrant" in specifying the particular function in question. All initiated believers are celebrants in liturgy. The avoidance of gender implications indicates the author's hope and confidence that women will be accepted for ordination in churches which until now have theologically justified the cultural barriers against them (instead of witnessing to the human liberation and the human unity of the reign of God and challenging those barriers).

One will find no reference to a practice called "concelebration" in the following pages, so a note of explanation is in order. This is a manual on presiding in liturgy, and presiding is a function for one person in a group. How any other clergy present participate in a liturgical celebration is quite another problem. The current practice in many churches of vesting such other clergy and inviting them to stand together in a central location, doing some of the texts and gestures of the presider in an unpracticed choral fashion, is problematic. The liturgical problem is twofold, at least: 1) they have no necessary function in the rite and therefore might be considered to be among those superfluities which a firm, strong, clean ritual action abhors; 2) because they have no necessary function they tend to accent, visually and experientially, the separation of clergy from church, a separation which will be discussed in this manual as one of the principal obstacles to an improved style of presiding.

We are in the early stages of a profound church renewal, which will include a renewal of ministries. Wherever the rethinking of ministries may lead us on this question, the concerns of this manual are strictly those of a single presider and a single act of presiding. In any case, this is the regular and ordinary experience of most participants in Christian liturgy. Meanwhile, for the sake of all *baptized* concelebrants in liturgical action, let any baptized-and-ordained concelebrants assess their participation (including *the way it looks*) with an orthodox theology of ministries that stresses function more than power and service more than status. Mass stipends, of course, where they still exist, are an important and fundamental part of this problem.

The focus of this manual is the ordinary Sunday celebration in most local church units, so its thrust is not directed to the small neighborhood or livingroom celebration. Common sense, especially about the appropriateness of any of its concrete suggestions, will take care of any such adaptations.

Finally, a word about the limits of any book that aspires to be an aid to better presiding. Readers will note in these pages a keen sense of the limits of verbalization, words, instruction, pedagogy, along with an emphasis on the nonverbal, symbolic, body language of liturgy. It is fighting fire with fire to try to communicate a feeling for these problems through a book. As long as we recognize that any guidebook must suffer these built-in limitations, our use of it will be realistic and modest.

It can't reach out and give your arm a squeeze, which might do more for your presiding style than anything we can print. It cannot visualize, for visual and television people, the sort of presiding it keeps talking about. It can, however, through its words, attempt to stir up some enthusiasm for the job and some understanding of its requirements. It can attempt to induce appropriate feelings as well as sound ideas. It is chancy to try to do these things with words, but it is worth a try.

The Presider's Spirit

The trouble with the kind of genuine church renewal that we
have gotten ourselves into is that problems and questions *begin*
(deceptively) at a fairly superficial and manageable level. At first
it looks easy. And then, almost imperceptibly, each of the problems and questions invites us deeper and deeper into the heart
of ecclesial faith, where all their roots are intertwined.

The bad news and the good news in all of this are really the
same: none of the isolated questions or problems is soluble by
itself; they all go together. What seemed at the beginning to be
complex and to lend itself to the handles of our various special-
izations, proves to be quite simple, but calls for a conversion and
a total commitment. It is good to know that it all goes together,
even if the sum is greater and more burdensome than the parts.
The congruence of Jesus, gospel, church and faith with life's
experience is a forceful apologia.

That, simply, is the chief reason why a guidebook on presiding
in liturgy cannot commence with the "practical" details of techniques and mechanics. Important as these latter are, they are
not at the heart of the matter. These pages are concerned, first
of all, with a spirit, a consciousness, an awareness. With that
spirit, techniques are indispensable and highly useful. Without
that spirit, techniques are dangerous.

The presider's function, ordinarily a clergy function, has become
depersonalized over the course of many centuries. Persons could
perform them "with their eyes closed," so to speak. It is clear
in these early stages of basic ecclesial reform and renewal that
the new situation requires a radical break with habits and customs
of long (and "good") standing. A whole new job description is
involved. The presider's liturgical task, with its remote and
immediate preparation, is now a duty of first priority demanding
serious training, a heavy time allocation and a budget to match.

*Presiders liturgical
task.*

All-important context: church

Training, time and budget are not helpful without the spirit. One of the most important marks of the new spirit characterizing the renewal movement is a close attention to the local church (in the sense of local congregation or parish). Initiation into this community of faith, reconciliation among its members, its mutual support system or lack thereof—these are recognized increasingly by serious Christians as fundamental problems and related problems. The community of faith, the local church, when it focuses on its concrete reality, sees all sorts of strengths and weaknesses which are not evident as long as church is conceived chiefly in universal and abstract terms.

This attention to the local assembly of believers, the church in the concrete, is at the heart of the renewal effort among churches of Catholic tradition. The emphasis these churches have placed in past centuries on communion among the churches, and the relationships of the churches, with their episcopal college and presbyteral colleges, has been in many ways salutary and faithful to the gospel of peace. One does not have to minimize this value, or the compelling truth, goodness and beauty of this communion, in order to assert again the importance of the local church, on which all inter-church relationships depend.

So the local congregation is coming into its own as the sine qua non of a healthy Christian ecclesial life. The quality of any communion of churches or any worldwide church depends on the quality of its individual congregations as well as on the quality of their relationships with each other. We have to look at the church in the flesh, where it exists in actual assemblies of believers. If this group of living, breathing disciples who meet together on Sunday in this particular time and place—if this gathering is a weak church, it cannot help but affect the whole. If it is weak in its sharing of prayer and faith, of rite and mission, if it is weak in the way it brings new members in and sustains the old ones, if it is lacking bonds of friendship, encouragement and mutual support—then the whole church suffers and all the related churches suffer.

The church as minister

For our purposes in this manual, it is sufficient to note that the same attention to the local church has vast implications for any and all of the church's particular ministries. In other words, church comes first, the community of faith comes first, the assembly of the baptized comes first, and the fundamental reality of ministry is the ministry of the entire servant church. Specific ministries, ordained, commissioned, or simply recognized in the community, depend on the church, not vice versa. Specific ministries arise out of the needs of the church.

Basic to any real understanding of specific full or part time, professional or amateur ministries within the faith community is the feeling (not just the intellectual grasp but the *feeling*) that the whole church is ministerial, is ministry. It exists to be the servant of the world God loves. Baptism-confirmation-eucharist, the sacraments of initiation, are the basis of a common Christian vocation and call to be ministers and to minister.

Only when we have established, believed and felt that truth can we begin to consider with a right mind the specific ministries which the church needs at a given time and place for its life and mission. Since the church exists to serve humanity, especially in its suffering, despised, fringe and poor members, it seems clear that the community of faith, as minister, will make judgments and will act in ways that bring the judgment of the reign of God to bear on societal ways and institutions (although this is admittedly dreaming of future possibility rather than describing present reality). It will also employ people to meet needs which society in general either overlooks or is unable/unwilling to cope with. One group of specific ministries, therefore, will have responsibility for doing whatever the church considers (in its "sense of the meeting") it can do to meet these human needs. These works of ministry will not be viewed as "charities" in any philanthropic or pejorative sense but as simple requirements of the reign of God, the reign of justice and peace.

As the role of deacon historically attests, these social ministries need not be exclusive of liturgical ones, but it cannot be assumed that the existence of liturgical ministries takes care of any ministries specifically related to the church's service of the community at large, especially in deprived and oppressed members.

Since the church is constituted and regularly renewed or built up in sacramental liturgy, symbolic ritual action, this also means a number of specific ministries for ordering and carrying out those actions in a way that will maximize the experience, inspiration and participation of the faith community: bishops, pastors,

Specific ministries arise out of the needs of the church

Common Christian vocation

3

priests, and sometimes others to preside as the climax of a more total pastoral service to the local church; deacons to wed this liturgical service with the broader social ministry of the church; readers to proclaim; acolytes to assist; ushers to be hosts for the assembly; ministers of holy communion to be agents in the personal exchange dimension of sacramental action; preachers to reflect on scripture in the context of the real world; ministers of the arts, essential to the environment of worship as well as to the celebration; and other possible and/or occasional ministries to enable beautiful and lively and experiential celebrations.

Educational needs of the community of faith, for children and adults, imply other categories of ministries. Ecumenical relations among the still separated networks or communions of churches imply still others. One could go on. None of these specific ministerial functions is necessarily exclusive of another, but each requires certain aptitudes, training and time which not everyone in the congregation possesses or can give, and each must have assigned responsibility with corresponding authority and account-ability. Similar divisions of responsibilities and labor are inescap-able in any human and social activity.

All specific offices of responsibility, all ministries are expressions of the ministerial and servant nature of the entire community of faith, the whole local church. Because of past assumptions that every ministry must be better or worse, higher or lower than every other ministry, we find it difficult to appreciate this variety of talents, gifts and responsibilities. The world's competitive and comparative phobias overwhelm the gospel notion that such differences of function (which we need) are unrelated to categor-ies of superiority or inferiority (which we do not need). So it is not really a lovely thought, but it can seem to be, that, since everyone is a minister, no one should have a specific ministerial office with concrete authority and accountability. If one wants to bring the kingdom enterprise to a grinding halt, one can stop with that thought and bask in its dull glow.

Specific, concrete ministries assigned to individuals with apti-tude, training and desire, by ordination or by some other form of church commissioning—these are not substitutes for the inac-tion of other Christians, but are extensions of the faith commu-nity's action and ministry. They are hands and limbs which the body of the church uses to do those parts of its work which require special time, training, skill and support.

4

The mutuality at the heart of a Christian concept of ministry is beginning to be a part of the consciousness of those most involved in church renewal. If the community of faith enriches and brings something to the life of an individual through its delegate's act of sacramental or other ministry, it is also true that the individual in that encounter enriches and brings something to the life of the faith community and of the minister who represents it.

In other words, it would be insufficient (speaking, for example, of the act of sharing holy communion with a sick person) to point out that a sick person needs the presence and touch of the church through its sacramental minister, although that is true as far as it goes. One should, however, complete the thought and the reality of the situation by adding that the church and its minister need the experience, gifts and love of the sick person, also.

It may be natural for a pragmatic people to think of ministry and servanthood not as quality, disposition, spirit, attitude, but always as "ministry *to*" someone. The emphasis on *to* has diminished ministry. The other party becomes an object and a *terminus ad quem* rather than a living participant and another source. Presiders, like other specific liturgical ministers, need very much to know the congregation not merely as those who are served (although even that is better than knowing them as those who are dominated), but also as those who support and heal and encourage the presider and are active in the dialogue.

In finding ways to communicate their healing and supporting power, congregations have been as clumsy as their clergy. Cars, houses, good meals, vacation trips, gratuities of various sorts—all are attempts to communicate something to those who serve them. One of the fruits of renewal is the growing realization that that "something" (support, joined hands, mutuality, etc.) could be communicated more appropriately by way of other modalities.

The process of discovering and developing these other modalities, again, must be a mutual one. On the one hand, clergy who are firmly established *within,* rather than above, the church will find ways to support a great variety of ministries and vocations already operative in that community—persons doing different things in different situations, but with the same motive of faith-inspired service. On the other hand, Christians who are motivated by and find meaning in roles apparently unrelated to specific liturgical or other corporate ecclesial ministries will find ways to share their sense of accomplishment with those in such roles whose functioning has helped kindle and sustain their inspiration.

The erosion of enthusiasm which often accompanies the gaining of age and wisdom is not the problem of the presider alone. It is a problem of the whole faith community. A community that feels profoundly the importance of its liturgical celebrations for the inspiration and sustenance of its own life of faith, hope, love will have all its ministers responding to its vibrations. Likewise, clergy who feel the same thing will have an immense effect (out of proportion to anything they say or do, although not unrelated to what they say and do) on the entire congregation.

"Democratizing" or sensitizing?

While there may be some acceptability to be gained, there is much truth to be lost by casting the church's reform and renewal in the terms of political democracy. As a faith community, conscious of the Spirit's presence and seeking the Spirit's guidance, the church's business is to cultivate a consensus sensitivity rather than a majority vote psychology. Any time the church acts as church the aim should be a real feeling that all have been listened to and that all can act together in obedience to the word of the Lord rather than the majority. The aim should be what Friends call "the sense of the meeting" rather than a counting of 51 per cent.

The odds against such an aim are great: both our political climate and the ecclesiastically authoritarian background of many of us. But Christians simply cannot be satisfied with "democratizing." Our tradition has it that God sometimes speaks through the youngest, or the "least," or a minority. We have no right to hurry matters to "a vote." We have to take the time to make ourselves understood when differences arise, mellowing them with prayer and finding a truly common way.

The church's historical experience with monarchy and the havoc of monarchy's influence upon church life and ministries should have made us skeptical of any governmental model. We have been monarchicalized very thoroughly in our past. One would think we would hesitate a bit before speaking too gleefully about being democratized in our present. Democracy is certainly an improvement in governmental models, but it is far from consensus in the Spirit. Its majority can be as disdainful of the individual or the minority as any monarchy, and as cruel, and as oblivious to the voice of the Spirit.

This appropriate search for consensus finds its primary aids in two human activities which are uniquely ecclesial: common prayer and acceptance of the judgment of the gospel. An atmosphere of prayer does not eliminate the possibility of differences of opinion, but it does situate the holders of these differences on the same level—sisters and brothers, sinners, loved by God, humble, open to one another, recognizing their own limits. These are the kinds of feelings which enable a group to seek consensus decisions (which may not be unanimous but will be quite different from majority vote conclusions) in a realistic and human way.

Acceptance of the judgment of the gospel, again, offers the ecclesial community a great advantage in its pursuit of a "sense of the meeting." It means that we have a norm superior to our opinions, and that we are all in the same position with respect to that norm. Even if it is not always easy to explicate that norm in the case of each concrete issue, the milieu of obedience to God in which we find ourselves is very real, very intentional, unlike the milieu in which most human arguments take place.

Presiding in liturgy

With those brief and absolutely necessary preliminary remarks about church and about the whole church as minister and servant, we can get to the subject of this guidebook: the specific ministry of the presider in public worship. Like all other specific ministries assigned to individuals in the church, this important service is utterly unintelligible in isolation, apart from the basis and context of the entire faith community and its ministry.

Churches that have been preoccupied for centuries with other aspects of their corporate lives have taken the function, office, task of presiding in liturgy for granted. Not much time has been spent defining it. Not much thought has been given to aptitude and qualifications for its exercise. It has been widely assumed that whoever is ordained must be ready, and scrutinies before ordination are rarely concerned with what will be the candidate's most prominent activity after ordination.

Presiding is a service of leadership in a common and participatory action called "liturgy," therefore an action that with full intent and purpose is done in the presence of God. As "a service

Presiding is a service of leadership.

of leadership," it normally assumes an already existing relationship with the community assembled. Ordinarily one should not be leading people in an activity as deep and central and personal as their ritualizing about the meaning of their lives unless one has previously known them and served them in a role related to fundamental issues.

"In a common and participatory action" clearly implies a planned, coordinated, complex and choreographed action in which the leader must be in contact with other ministers and with all other parts of the assembly at all times, must know clearly and precisely where the action is going, and must be able to anticipate what is coming next.

That definition also requires a measure of trust and influence in the relationship between the presider and other participants in the assembly. Nowhere does a lack of personal involvement, conviction, enthusiasm show more clearly and more damagingly than in the leadership of a worshiping congregation. Everyone has experienced, in one public meeting or another, the corporate effect of discomfort and demoralization when the leader is patently without enthusiasm for, conviction about, or involvement in the meeting and its particular purposes.

Because liturgy is unique among human assemblies in its direct concern with ultimate issues and the totality of life, those defects in a leader are especially disheartening, even scandalizing, for the whole group. It is not a matter of anyone's passing judgment on the presider's feelings or intent. It is, rather, an inevitable reaction to the primary data at hand, to the observable facts: the way the presider looks and acts and sounds. A quiet enthusiasm and a conviction about the importance of liturgical action are assets that a presider can neither feign nor do without.

Presiding is a service required by any group of people who have gathered for a common purpose. When that purpose is common prayer in the tradition of people of biblical faith, that meeting is a liturgy. Presiding is, therefore, a service which liturgy requires. The term "presider" is accurate, even though it needs in any given time and place considerable elaboration. It is accurate because it states clearly and unequivocally a function which must be exercised by someone in a liturgical assembly. It is also theologically sound, because it depends on a gathering, an assembly of God's people, the church. No one is born a presider. No one is made a presider by training or talent or will or desire or anything but the choice and vocation and delegation of the faith community. There are certainly native aptitudes and basic training, but presiders, like all other ministers, are made by the church.

That is the beginning, but only the beginning. The training that precedes the church's ordination or delegation for this function has not yet caught up with the spirit or the needs of contemporary liturgical celebration. Except in situations where catechists or others substitute, the clergy ordinarily occupy the presider's chair. To this day in many places, the clergy are educated for all of their duties except this one—their most public and prominent function.

It is an extremely curious fact, but it is still a fact. Clergy education takes almost no account generally of what the clergy are supposed to be doing in those working hours when they are in public contact with most of the members of their churches. What they are supposed to be doing—and doing well—in those hours is dealing with and in the symbol language, body language, movement language, music language, action language, visual language, as well as with the spoken language of liturgy.

Clergy conferences and workshops are reflecting an awareness of these needs, and people are talking more about the inadequacy of theological school and seminary programs which fail to deal with symbol, sacrament and ritual in any but narrowly intellectual terms. So there is hope that things will change. But add these ecclesial problems to the general culture's rationalistic and pragmatic bias (which so discourages a human attention to art and beauty and contemplation and things-in-themselves), and you have a scene that is bleakest in those areas most essential to good liturgical celebration and to the fulfillment of the presider's role with competence and style.

In Christianity's climactic and central liturgy, the eucharist, the presider's function has not only a local dimension—ordering and leading enthusiastically this particular congregation's sacramental action—but also another dimension, relating this celebration to the eucharistic celebrations of the other churches and to those churches as communities of faith. This is why in churches of Catholic tradition, the presider must be a bishop or priest in

How one comes to be a presider.

Presiders made by the church.

Presiding and priorities

9

collegial relationship with the other churches (through the episcopal or presbyteral college to which the presider belongs). Sometimes this relationship is expressed in the turgid, legal language of validity and liceity, sometimes in the richer Christian terms of communion and personal symbolism. In any case, an understanding of this dimension is necessary for an understanding of current eucharistic practice, given the appalling fact of Christian failure to achieve even the loose and variety-respecting kind of church unity which gospel-oriented Christians desire.

While it will be obvious that many of the statements and suggestions in this book have the eucharistic liturgy in mind, the book is directed to the role of the presider in any kind of liturgy —any form of public, common prayer. The hope of The Liturgical Conference is that other types of liturgies will soon be more common in those churches whose sole practical experience of public worship is with the eucharist. The eucharist is the summit and climax, the central rite, and it needs the support, variety and formative spiritual preparation not only of private and family prayer but also of other forms of common prayer in the faith community.

Qualifications of a presider

Renewal has us sorting out our tradition, getting a grasp of the essentials again, reestablishing gospel priorities. This process is revealing, bringing into the light a number of problems, among them the fact that the qualifications of candidates for ministries need an extremely critical examination. This is to be expected at a time which finds the whole church rediscovering itself and its authentic face under some layers of camouflage. Naturally, then, agelong clerical traditions, customs, rules, habits, ways are now subject to a scrutiny more fundamental and intense than anything they have known in centuries.

With a renewed emphasis on ministerial function (rather than on ministry as a class, status, caste or rank), churches that have retained the male and celibate qualifications are wondering how much the confusion of ministerial office with a kind of ecclesial upper class has had to do with the retention. They wonder, too, whether an historical cultural situation, now rapidly changing, was not primarily responsible for reserving the clerical function to the male of the species. While the economic argument for celibacy remains evident, a more positive view of human sexuality among Christian thinkers and moralists contributes to a growing challenge to that Western custom.

Historians can illuminate the genesis of the monk as the model for all clergy, but it certainly happened sometime and it endured. Celibacy became identified with clerical service in the West and with the office of bishop in the East. Of these, as of all clerical customs, it must be said that the living church has given and the living church can take away. If ministries themselves arise from the living church and its needs, then certainly even the most venerable qualifications for candidates are less than eternal. Any bishop who speaks on this subject at this time without reference to the tremendously significant questioning and soul-searching and reevaluation going on is not taking the collegial nature of his office very seriously. This, rather than the positions taken, seems to cast a shadow on the pope's recent correspondence with the archbishop of Canterbury on the subject of women in the priesthood.

The economic advantage of cheap labor is something of a fiction. Clerical labor is costly like all labor, but the costs are hidden frequently and the paper salary is low. This tends to perpetuate unhappy patterns of clerical life and income and tends to make any real reform in ordained ministries depend upon a salary scale attuned to the economic realities of the day. Until salaries are realistic, open and honest, the fight against clergy problems like paternalistic patronage, simony and tax-dodging will continue to be uphill.

As a consequence of the fact that exceptions to celibacy among Western churches in communion with Rome are extremely rare, we have a tremendous reservoir of unused pastoral talent and experience in men who have resigned without losing their desire to serve in clergy roles. One cannot prepare a guidebook for presiders at this time in history without noting this loss to the churches, grave harm to the persons involved, and without lamenting our apparent inability to deal with the problem in a humanly satisfactory way. We are old hands at being at variance with gospel values, but our rigidity in this matter is a particularly striking instance.

Dominant culture, economic patterns and social pressures also impose (this time in *all* the churches) other qualifications which though not a matter of law, are effective in making sure that most clergy in what dominant groups in the U.S. call "the main traditions" are white Anglos, middle class, middle of the road. This is changing, with a slowly increasing recognition of the black and hispanic presence. The danger again is that minority groups and what society would call "fringe groups" are inadequately represented among those groups of clergy. As in the case of women's exclusion from clerical roles, the particular gifts, talents, sensitivities of minorities and non-mainstream elements in the society are also lost to those offices of leadership in most of the churches. With our ingrained racism and white dominance added to the already overbearing weight of social pattern, it is necessary to go out of our way to encourage their representation, for the sake of everyone's freedom and enrichment.

Because all of these fairly irrelevant qualifications for the presider's office have loomed so large in the past and have captured the attention of the church whenever ministry is in question, it is critically important for the office of presider as well as for other ministries to assert strongly and affirmatively a series of qualifications for ministries that are relevant to the functions under consideration. Appropriate qualifications for the ordained clergy (particular places and times may add others) are: 1) depth and commitment of faith; 2) native talent, especially the particular and crucial talent of openness to others, respect for the charisms of others, and willingness to share responsibility with others as "one who cares"; 3) desire and feeling of call; 4) adequate training for the function in question; 5) accomplishment or proved aptitude in apprenticeship; 6) a call and mandate from a church, a faith community; and, finally, 7) a commitment to continuing education.

Belief and prayerfulness

While these qualifications seem to be the obvious ones, they will appear differently in every candidate, and one can never dispense with the judgment of the faith community and persons representing it. The first of them requires further comment here; the others are either susceptible only of personal examination or clearly specified by the demands of liturgical presidency as discussed in the rest of this guidebook.

"Depth and commitment of faith" is a very broad qualification, but at minimum it suggests personal belief that is real and meaningful and operative, and a disposition to prayer, especially prayer of praise and thanksgiving. This kind of faith is even more fragile than human life, and its indispensability in the pastoral office is a cogent reason for making resignations from the clergy more easy and less threatening than they have been generally. These qualities are closely bound up with feelings of awe, mystery, the holy, reverence, which simply have to be present in the one who presides in liturgical celebration. Admittedly, those feelings take different forms in different cultural scenes, but there is something about them that crosses such boundaries and is universally recognizable. The best of presiding techniques appear shrill, pretentious, self-assertive and empty without this qualification. The worst techniques are made bearable (if not delectable) by its presence.

In the liturgical assembly we are striving to be at the height of our God-consciousness, and therefore of our human-consciousness. It is an awesome thing to face the mystery of the Other and the mystery of ourselves with such purpose and intent. It is intolerable that such an assembly should be led by a person who has no apparent interest in the proceedings, or by a person who seems to be using the situation to dominate, or to display, or to collect the plaudits of a crowd.

The inflation of the clergy

Aim and aspiration are terribly important, even though we do not always hit the mark. We are limited by our humanity and by our history. No human being can ever really "begin at the beginning." Every social configuration from the family into which one is born to the most complex of our institutions is a bundle of traditions, customs, ways, habits, rules and laws. We may use these bundles or we may be oppressed by them, but their pervasive presence is never an option. They are always a given, and inescapable. This is one reason why conversion is such a shattering and traumatic event, and why it needs the support of a strong, initiating community of faith. Conversion is as close as we can come to a new beginning, because it rejects some and questions all of the social givens by which our lives have been supported in the past.

Just as we have discovered that many "liturgical" problems are really problems concerning the faith community in its formation and total life, so a lot of questions which may seem to be about presiding turn out to involve more general clergy profiles, images and customs. The chair of the presider, for example, is rarely seen as only that: the symbol and the seat of an essential role in our gathering for common prayer. No, our history intervenes, and makes the chair for us the symbol also of all that we remember about the clergy, good and bad, positive and negative, loveable and hateful. No wonder we have so much difficulty with a relatively simple piece of furniture.

It has been said that as the sacraments of initiation (baptism, confirmation, eucharist) declined in popular importance and eventfulness the gap thus created was filled by an expansion and inflation of ordination and religious profession. As the former rites suffered diminishment, the latter grew out of proportion. As the life of the Christian in the church became common, humdrum, ordinary, people began to think of and look at the clergy and those living in vows as if they alone were the genuine, 100% believers.

While that may not be a terribly surprising development, it is one that is extremely damaging to the self-understanding of the whole church. We should have known, and been on guard against it. Instead we encouraged it. We set the clergy in countless ways (physically, mentally, emotionally, spiritually) apart from the communities for whose service they were ordained. Even the training of candidates became at times a systematic alienation from the total life of the church in the world.

Cyrille Vogel describes a fundamental cause of this separation of ordained ministers from the concrete faith community in *Liturgy: Self-Expression of the Church* (Concilium, ed. Herman Schmidt, Herder & Herder, 1972, p. 19). Speaking of the ancient tradition governing ordination, he says: "The clergy (bishop, presbyter, deacon) have meaning and reality only by virtue of their rootedness in the community as ministers of the word and of sacramental life . . . If the ordained man is not appointed to a specific office of service in the community, ordination (even when carried out according to the prescribed rules and rites) is null and void (not only illicit or annulable); this is the ordination which our texts call 'absolute,' in the sense of being without any ministerial reference. An ordination conferred without any precise pastoral mission, or upon the individual as such, is unreal." That is the ancient Catholic tradition.

Vogel continues: "All the available evidence agrees that this was doctrine and practice until approximately the end of the twelfth century. Since that time, but *only since then* . . . , any ordination, provided that it is carried out in accordance with the rites as set forth in the official liturgical books, remains valid, even if it is absolute and conferred outside any consistent community. This change, at the end of the twelfth century, has as its major consequence a complete uprooting and dissociation of the clergy from the church."

Those are strong words: "a complete uprooting and dissociation of the clergy from the church." Our current problems, however, tell us that they are not too strong. This process of clerical estrangement from the faith community in no way implies a lack of dedication or of a desire to serve on the part of clergy generally. The inflation of their own and others' ideas of their independence in relation to the concrete church and of their importance was not sought in any deliberate way. It just happened.

The bitter taste came later, when we began to notice that most Christians were speaking of "the church" as "they," not "we." The bitter taste was sensed when "the church" appeared to be commonly felt as an outside force, an external institution to which we must somehow conform. Underneath that little, apparently innocuous slip of the tongue ("they," rather than "we") lay mindsets, attitudes, customs jelled and hardened over the course of centuries into *distance* between most of the baptized, on the one hand, and their clergy servants, on the other. A lot has been done and is being done to curb this inflation and to bridge this gap. But the chasm is still very much a major obstacle in the work of presiding in liturgy.

The high price of "Christendom"

At least some of this distance between clergy and the rest of the baptized can be traced to cultural forces beyond the faith community. Christopher Dawson may have been correct when he attributed the West's revolutionary spirit and its striving for human progress to the spark and power of biblical faith. But it is also true that when Western powers gave their cultural blessing to the Christian faith and church, they simultaneously and thoroughly domesticated the ecclesial institution and extracted most of its prophetic teeth.

One of the ways to tame the kingdom witness of the church is surely to make its pastoral leaders as pleased as they can be with whatever political and economic situation prevails in a given time and place. Privileges and exemptions of various sorts, appearances on public platforms and seats with the mighty, a good press, an indulgent police—these are a small price for the political and economic bosses of any society to pay for a docile, or at least benevolent episcopate and presbyterate. No conspiracy is involved, not even anything that technically can be called a bribe—that's only doing what comes naturally.

So it is that the mighty have a subtle control even over our singing about their being deposed (as we do quite regularly in liturgical celebrations). The price is higher for the church, since those societal privileges further separate the clergy from the rest of the faithful and measurably reduce the prophetic and critical spirit of the latter as well as the former. A church that simply conforms to the culture ceases to be church. As eschatological sign, it must witness to the tension between what human society is at any given moment and what the will of God invites that culture to become.

For some reason not entirely to their credit, the baptized have generally seemed to favor cultural privileges for their members who are clergy. And what has softened the tongue of professional preachers has rendered pliable the consciences of most Christians. Instead of anamnesis (remembering, for example, the model of ministerial leadership in the New Testament), we find ourselves with a kind of amnesia, in which culture's leadership roles overwhelm that model. There is a special ugliness about a function of humble service (which any vocation or work must be, in order to be fit for a Christian) that has become a symbol of superiority or even a tool of power and domination. One thinks of the old Latin proverb, *corruptio optimi pessima,* which Tom Quigley has translated, "Trivialize a strong concept and you'll end up with cotton candy."

The cotton candy that has sometimes passed for episcopal and presbyteral service is the manner and attitude of a prince. Always a strong temptation for people in offices of leadership, that manner and attitude are disastrous in the church. It really doesn't matter whether the motive is selfish or unselfish. The effects are the same: an isolated person, patronizing, condescending, evoking sentiments of fear, resentment, irresponsibility, apathy, indifference, servility in the faith community. Calling those sentiments by the noble names of "obedience" or "respect" does not, unfortunately, change their character.

The way the presider views that ministry is as important as the way the congregation views it. Inflated notions of clerical rank, illusions of independence from the community, the "pet" psychology that accounts for paternalism toward the clergy by the rich and the powerful—these poison the whole atmosphere, whether they come from one source or another. They make it impossible to preside in liturgy with truth, with faithfulness and with dignity.

One more note about an historical problem before we get to the "practical" part. The liturgical celebrations of a community of faith, by the demands of both tradition and common sense, require several active ministerial roles (apart from the congregation's) to carry as well as to vary the ritual action. Liturgical development and tradition seem to push for a variety of persons and roles in every celebration: presider, musicians, readers, acolytes, etc. They simply do not envision a single person facing the entire assembly.

So the presider has a function with regard to the other ministers as well as to the assembly as a whole. The presider facilitates, discreetly yields the focus to the one who is operating at a particular moment, guides, prompts when necessary, leads the congregation in attending to the action. This is not easy for clergy who have become accustomed to "doing everything." When the presider does everything except those parts of the liturgy which belong to the entire congregation, we have a kind of liturgical barbarism. Where, then, are the talents and the gifts and the competencies of the community? Where is the recognition of the alternations and rhythms of ritual action? It is a kind of minimalism, an "efficiency" that militates against everything that liturgical renewal stands for.

A variety of functioning individual ministers in a liturgical celebration *is not*: 1) extraordinary; 2) supererogatory; 3) a sop for the activists and potential trouble-makers in the congregation; 4) a means of forcing the ministerial involvement of Christians who are not clergy; 5) a device for filling the empty chairs up

**Other ministers
and the presider**

Presider – facilitates

front; 6) an effort to relieve the loneliness of a presider who is uncomfortable with the congregation.

Employment of a variety of ministers belongs to the nature of liturgical action—this is the fact of the matter, and clergy who do not appreciate it are incapable of presiding well. As a community action, good liturgy seeks to utilize the different abilities represented in the congregation. As a moving action, one of the ways liturgy defines its parts is by having different functions performed by different persons. As the church's sacrifice of praise, liturgy gives space and attention to the various gifts of the Spirit in God's people. As a familiar, ritual action, liturgy involves everyone, alternating persons and groups of persons, each with something special to do. Besides all this, interest in any human event will depend to some extent on not always confronting the same face in the spotlight.

And then the beauty of it

The beauty and nobility of this office, or function, or service, is so great that the church's call to its exercise should be an overwhelming experience for anyone, veteran or novice. To lead in public worship, in the ritual play of a faith community, is more gift than burden. Its beauty and nobility are in its service as a facilitator of liturgical celebration, which is: 1) unique in the life of the church, since it both constitutes and sustains the faith community; 2) indispensable in a church which serves humanity by being a sign of the reign of God and therefore needs to ritually create a kingdom scene for its vision and refreshment; 3) humanly necessary to relax the tight grip of the status quo, so that people can move and breathe and envision alternatives.

When Christians generally begin to see the liturgical action as their responsibility (the planning and the celebrating of it) and as a uniquely significant human event, then the one who presides will begin to feel the service value, the excitement and the witnessing power of that function. Nowhere else is one so much a healer in every sense as in facilitating this ritual play of a faith community.

Who is there of any age or maturity who does not understand that what meets the eye in human life—our ways, customs, institutions—is so determiningly powerful, so totally pervasive that any message of radical sisterhood and brotherhood is up against it from the start? Life meets every proclamation, every vision, every hope with its facts. And the facts box us in so closely that only in recent years have ordinary people even begun to feel that they can control (rather than be controlled by) political and economic powers.

All the while liturgy has maintained its subtle but relentless witness against the facts of life. All the while liturgy, however powerless it has seemed in the struggle for justice and peace, has kept alive a kingdom vision and what anthropologists like Victor Turner call a threshold or liminal perspective that refuses to be imprisoned by those facts. This is no small service to the human race. And to preside in the very deed that so expands the life of creatures is a function of unquestionable beauty and nobility.

The Presider's Role in Planning

Planning is neither a luxury nor a discovery of recent decades. Planning has always been necessary for good liturgical celebration, and the involvement of the presider in planning has always been necessary not only for the good of the group process but also for competence in presiding. A good presider must be fully aware of what is going to happen at every planned moment in the course of a celebration.

Even in the days when some took it for granted that the whole of liturgy was prepackaged and sealed up in a book, there was a lot of planning going on among serious clergy who respected the importance of common prayer—planning about homilies, congregational involvement, symbols, actions, movements, environment, etc. Then it was commonly done privately, or with other clergy. There wasn't as much thought about options, adaptations, spontaneity as there is now. But there certainly was planning.

There were also some, however, who felt that it was all there in the book. They did not choose to plan, preferring to devote their work time to matters less germane to the clerical calling. They developed a habit of approaching the task of presiding armed with nothing but the book and perhaps a few ideas about the homily. That this habit is still widespread, if not dominant, can hardly be doubted by anyone who has any kind of broad experience of the quality of most contemporary celebrations.

Whatever may be said about some of the liturgical books of the past few centuries, the liturgical books of every tradition now require planning. They provide a normative and vital contact with tradition. They offer structures and patterns of ritual action tried by history. They indicate rhythms and alternations and meanings which we ignore at our peril. But they also make demands: they demand incarnation and realization and celebration in the heart of the contemporary human scene; they demand the living flesh and blood choices and adaptations and creative

**Planning—
a sine qua non**

activity of a concrete church, a faith community, real people. Only when they come to life in the action of an assembly of believers and in conjunction with the needs and feelings of a certain time and place do the texts and rubrics of the book become liturgy.

And that takes planning. This book is about presiding, not about planning as such. For the latter concerns, the other periodicals and books of The Liturgical Conference will be useful, especially *Liturgy Committee Handbook,* the rest of the ministry series mentioned on the back of the title page of this volume, *From Ashes to Easter—Design for Parish Renewal, Major Feasts and Seasons,* and the older *Manual of Celebration.* In the planning part of this volume, stress is on the place in the planning process of the one who will preside at the celebration.

The presider in the process

Normally, current liturgy planning is done in a small group situation. Even in cases where a congregation has a full or part time liturgy director, there is great value in the representation of felt needs and of particular competencies which a small planning group permits. Planning groups may be set up for a season in smaller parishes, for each particular hour of celebration during a season in larger parishes, for special festivals, etc. They should include some representation of different sectors in the congregation, as well as resource persons in liturgy, music and the other arts. A five or six person group—most advantageous for getting the work done—means that not every recognizable interest in the congregation will be represented in every group, but overall there can be a broad representation.

In this picture, the presider ordinarily will have the responsibility of being the resource person in liturgy, although in some cases there may be another available who has engaged in liturgical studies. It would be unfortunate, however, if that were the only felt reason for the presider's participation in planning.

The presider must be keenly aware of and thoroughly familiar with both the structure and the individual parts of the celebration. This is not the kind of awareness and familiarity that is gained by five minutes in the sacristy with the chief planner before the service starts. And even the best "master of ceremonies" is no substitute for the confidence and assurance of the one who presides. That is why the presider needs to participate in the planning group even when there is another resource person in liturgy available.

Secondly, of course, is the usefulness of the presider as resource person, serving the rest of the planners by communicating a real feeling for the basic structures and rhythms of traditional liturgical services. The clergy do not always have the benefit of adequate training in this area, so a reading program is essential— one that includes the liturgical books, commentaries on them, and pastoral interpretations. It helps, too, to look around one's region and seek to share especially good liturgical experiences where they can be found.

Even though secondary from the presider's point of view, the role of the liturgy resource person is critical in any planning group. Because we are dealing with liturgy, with a symbol language rooted in nature and history and developed in a long biblical and ecclesial tradition. Our present awkwardness embraces, at one end of the spectrum, congregations which attempt to use the liturgical books as if the books were the liturgy, fearful of every invitation to creativity, mechanical about options, and, at the other end, congregations who try every Sunday to reinvent the church, beginning from scratch, as if nothing had been learned in the past.

Both of these extremes act as if liturgical rites were random juxtapositions of various parts. The first group idolizes the parts as found in the books, assumes all have equal importance and indispensability, and misses the point: that they are there to serve more important meanings and experiences. The latter group seems to suppose that the parts are all equally disposable, that they can be omitted, ignored, rearranged at will, without any norms for the structure (to say nothing of the stability and familiarity) required in ritual action if it is to be humanly satisfying and functional.

There is little that is random about the movement and structure, the ebb and flow of liturgies. It is ignorance rather than bravery which must be held accountable for the failure of some liturgy planners to accept the responsibility inherent in our new freedom. Freedom to plan and adapt, to create a celebration,

A crucial service

to contribute to a living tradition—this involves responsibility greater than Christians have known for centuries.

We have moved to a deeper level of operation—a level that requires planning and preparation and real responsibility to tradition as well as to the circumstances of the times. Until current renewal efforts, we were operating (most of us) on a more superficial level. We had learned to expect a kind of liturgical uniformity everywhere. Wherever you happened to "drop in" (and those were the days when one "dropped in" to a liturgy . . . they *have* passed, haven't they?), you were supposed to hear the same words and music, see the same gestures and movements, etc. It was the old tourist argument. Or the shopping center chapel syndrome carried to its logical, anti-ecclesial conclusion.

Now we have deeper expectations, which are both more difficult and more possible. Now what we seek when we join with a strange community, an unfamiliar church, for common prayer is not to see and hear the same thing, necessarily, but to find among them the same experience of drawing our lives together before God, of mystery and praise, of the kingdom alternative, of faith and hope and love. The people of that foreign congregation can share this experience with us only if it is, first, real to them, in their idiom, with their talents, related to the stuff of their daily lives.

On this deeper level, it is more important than ever that the structures and the rhythms of the rites be understood. Without that competency and that feeling, planners can become arbitrary quite unwittingly. And their carelessness can be damaging to the liturgical experience of the people in ways so subtle that one doesn't realize what is happening until the damage has been done. Examples of some of these problems will appear later in this book.

Presider as listener

Tradition is only part of the planning group's responsibility. We also have to have people who are in close touch with the human scene at this time in this place, with people's problems and hopes and needs and aspirations and the way these relate to Jesus' message of liberation and solidarity in God. Those who have studied the ancestor of our eucharistic prayer, the ancient Jewish prayer form called *berekah*, tell us that it was not only praise, blessing, thanksgiving for God's great deeds and covenant, but also an interpretation of that covenant in terms of the people's current political and economic situation.

Presumably the presider will be an active participant in political and cultural life, although, unless clerical customs change very rapidly, the economic scene (which determines political and cultural life to such a great extent) is less familiar. Listening to those who are in it and of it—its critics as well as its beneficiaries and advocates—is essential if the presider is to have any competence in the pastoral adaptation of liturgies.

The norm here, of course, is the reign of God, its justice, its peace—the kingdom as an alternative to the status quo—and its judgment on current ways and institutions. The more one is beholden to current ways and institutions, the less one is capable of a kingdom witness. Freedom from captivity by the powers that be is, therefore, as important as listening. That is one of the reasons why a reform in clergy salaries and in the church's handling of its money and property in general is so central in the renewal process.

Then there is the listening one must do in the presence of musicians and other artists, whose contributions to liturgical celebrations are indispensable. This does not mean a surrender of pastoral priorities. It may mean a reassessment of just what those priorities should be. To defend pastoral priorities and to see that they are never overridden is simply to do one's pastoral duty. Liturgy is for people, and so are the arts which serve liturgy.

But art *is* a pastoral priority, even when there is no popular demand. Like prophecy, it is part of the church's business. We must attend to art because art affects us all—it makes us feel better or worse about ourselves and about what we are doing. Mere efficiency will never do for any human activity, least of all for liturgy.

A priest involved in planning for the Eucharistic Congress in Philadelphia in 1976 commented on the concern for "simplicity" voiced by Congress spokespersons in the course of some meetings. The latter judged that if the bishops wore anything grand in the way of vesture it would be an affront to poor people. The priest, who belonged to a minority group which has suffered both slavery and poverty in this country, laughed. If the bishops in question were *their own, belonged to them,* he said, poor people, like other people, would delight in the splash of grand vesture. He concluded, sadly, that when the bishops are clearly not theirs, any vesture, any presence is an affront.

Art is not for the kingdom, it is for this world that is in travail, that hasn't yet learned to share its wealth, that needs art's touch of beauty and goodness and truth. To reduce everything that is made for human public and communal use to the cheapest and the shoddiest is no service to poor people. It is a distraction from the fundamental social, political, economic reforms which Christians should be about. Meanwhile, if we are going to make things at all, we should try to make them humanly and rightly, and, therefore, with great care and reverence for art.

But, as we have seen, our culture is unfriendly to the arts in many ways, and unprepared to admit their vast importance and deep influence in human life. So we pay for plumbing, heating, lighting without a murmur, but when it comes to paying for music or the other arts we need in order to celebrate fittingly and well, we prefer to do without or to accept only that which is freely volunteered.

Planning which does not face these facts and find means to invite the best music and art available to serve liturgical celebration is not planning at all, but merely a custodial service. It is "economies" like this that deprive the faith community of those things that can make the difference between a dull and lifeless celebration and one that is ennobling and exciting. Suicide is also economical.

The problem of fear

All members of a planning group share responsibility for creating an atmosphere of love, acceptance and trust. The presider's pastoral role in the community adds emphasis and urgency to that general responsibility. The problem can be stated simply: love, acceptance, trust facilitate the planning process; fear and repression inhibit and corrupt that process.

These principles apply to relations both within the local congregation and between the local congregation and the wider diocese or body of churches. They appear to be truisms, but the history of Christianity proves that they are not. Only when church leaders, bishops, pastors are *not* anxious, insecure, uninformed in a particular area can functions involving coresponsibility in that area be handled properly.

In liturgy, a repressive climate (which is ordinarily a combination of authoritarianism and anxiety) condemns any progress in renewal as hopeless from the start. Instead of dealing with the relevant questions of quality and appropriateness and suitability, every adaptation and creative suggestion is stymied by irrelevant and futile considerations: "What will so-and-so say? or think? or do?" So the group is bogged down in the loser's course of anticipated rejection. That is worse than real rejection, because it not only halts action but it halts it without reason.

The churches that find fear and repression a great problem are those in which an authoritarian model has dominated church thinking and acting for an extended period of time. It is not difficult to understand. One can even sympathize. Churches that grew rapidly as a result of heavy immigration, with people crowded together in units large enough to support schools and with little thought of liturgical requirements, tended to look for sharp administrators to lead them. The accent was not on pastoral gifts. The search was for other talents.

So they found themselves in a position where many of their clergy, presiding regularly in liturgical celebration, viewed that ministry as merely a necessary part of a job whose focal points and priorities lay elsewhere. One might have hoped that the gradual rejection of the administrative model would lead to renewed focus on the liturgical office. This has not yet happened noticeably, although it may some time in the future. Liturgy suffered in the past from this neglect and it is suffering in the present.

A human sense of limits, enabling us to admit that we can err and make mistakes, is a healthy antidote to the inflated expectations that inhibit many of us almost as much as our fears. To strive for quality is not the same as to cultivate the illusion that our work can be perfect. One of the strengths of a ritual tradition is that it is capable of bearing up under great accumulations of mistakes and well-meant follies. If history tells us anything, it tells us that.

Some of the hurdles

Experience has proved to those who have spent many hours in planning groups that, even with the procedures recommended in the publications cited earlier in this book, certain obstacles or hurdles present themselves regularly. We cannot discuss the planning process here in any detail, but a presider who is aware of major hurdles can forewarn the chairperson. The latter can be prepared to handle the situation. Here are a few that have occurred frequently in this author's experience:

1. *The lure of a "theme."* The new Roman eucharistic rite provides a place for a minister to make a statement introductory to the day's celebration, after the presider's greeting and before the sprinkling. This, where it is practiced, is usually a brief statement of theme. Even apart from this, the theme idea is popular among planning groups. If properly understood, this is quite natural, since it is found in the church's year of feasts and seasons and in all standard lectionaries. Properly understood, the theme is a modest attempt to capture in a few sentences a message in the readings in the context both of the year and of the local human situation.

However, the theme gets out of hand more frequently than one would wish. It happens in at least these three ways: a) when the theme is separated from the year, season, or feast and from the lectionary, so that, instead of drawing it out of the scriptural word, we impose it from the outside, so to speak, on the celebration; b) when a theme is used to so dominate the entire celebration that every text and song and act must conform to it, and the celebration becomes a mere pedagogical tool; c) when the planning group luxuriates in the theme and spends its time homilizing about the theme rather than planning the liturgical celebration.

Blessing God with thanks and praise is the fundamental and sufficient theme for any liturgical celebration. Ritual traditions and structures guide us in doing this with respect to different human needs, events, situations. The scriptural word properly has a certain priority and initiative in public worship. After these considerations, and recognizing their primacy, then if we want to state a modest little particular theme, so be it. It can be helpful, if we keep it down to size, very brief, and subservient to the basic theme of all worship, to the rite, and to scripture.

2. *The lure of rationalism and pragmatism.* Because of training and pastoral function, the presider would be in a better position than most of the planning group to play the clown, the jester, to be the figure that relieves our celebration of the heavy

and omnipresent status quo. Part of that status quo is certainly a preoccupation with the word, the thought, the idea, and a consequent ignorance and lack of interest concerning the arts and what they can do for celebration. Music is critically important and essential in liturgical celebration, yet planning groups commonly treat it as an after thought, providing neither budget nor respect for competence. The same is true of the arts dealing with environment and with the furnishings, objects, symbols used in celebration.

A presider who feels the freedom of that role, then, can help make planning groups sensitive to the alienation of artists and craftspeople from the churches, and to the resulting impoverishment of liturgy. Even when, as in our culture generally, we are uninformed, uninterested and ignorant with respect to music and the other arts, we are nevertheless powerfully influenced by what we hear, see, and sense in other ways. The trouble is, most of us are unaware of this influence, even though we feel it, so we tend to blame bad liturgical experiences on the things we are conscious of: language, the content of texts or homily, etc. But if the aural and visual experience of a celebration were strong and beautiful and compelling, most of us wouldn't remember what the text was.

This particular obstacle and hurdle in the planning process can be dealt with if the members (including the presider) of the group are humble enough to seek competence and to give competence both authority and support (financial as well as moral). The rewards will be great, and one day the group will look back and wonder how it could have been satisfied with so much in the way of music, artifacts, utensils, furnishings that were unworthy of liturgical use—so much that was cheap, tawdry, sentimental, careless, inferior and incompetent.

3. The lure of planning out of context. This problem is related to the lure of themes (above), but it is so important that it deserves special consideration. Every liturgical celebration of a faith community takes place in the context not only of a certain kind of human situation but also of a particular year and season. The year is centered around Easter and the rhythms of nature. The seasons are variously oriented, but all in relation to Easter, and their specific moods and characteristics are enriching and humanly satisfying.

A particular celebration planned without reference to season and year, or to an adjacent feastday, is like a family gathering without memory or future, without any provision for the corporate experience of the different kinds of feelings humans have. It is no accident that gatherings of families or clans are usually related to seasons and feasts, so it is not surprising that liturgical celebrations which ignore the mood, the references, and the context of season exhibit a dreadful sameness and sterility.

4. The lure of the complex. Unless planning groups begin with the essentials of any particular liturgy, including sacrosanct past and established practice, they can quickly become tangled up in a labyrinth of fairly irrelevant gimmicks, frills and superficial remedies. The simplest, most basic essentials in a liturgical celebration are usually the most significant and often the most overlooked. A booklet on the celebration of baptism came to this author's desk a few years ago: it was full of suggestions about peripheral aspects of the celebration; it said nothing at all about the actual bathing, the washing with water.

If, for example, in planning a eucharistic celebration, a group brings in a combo of musicians for song support, a batch of slides to help create an environment, a troup of mime or dance specialists to illustrate the reading of the gospel, and does nothing about the bread and wine, it would not be unreasonable to send them all to bed without their suppers. In the eucharist, bread and wine are basic: their visual and other sensory impact, how they are handled, how they are broken and poured out, how shared. . . . But, because we are accustomed to a symbolic minimalism with respect to all sacraments, we tend to think that we have to bring in all sorts of entirely new elements to save this wretched rite. We make our problems more complex than they are. If we attended to the bread and wine, we would discover that the rite is powerful indeed.

Ethnic resources

If many Americans feel, as they obviously do, that they must go to the East for spiritual relief, it is only partly because of the intellectual and rationalistic biases of the churches of the West. It is also because the dominant white Anglo-Northern European types in most of the large U.S. churches are victims of a profound racism which effectively isolates them from those areas of Amer-

ican black and hispanic culture most relevant to our problems of
liturgical celebration.

This is not a "liberal" plea, but a statement of deprivation. A
personal note might be helpful in trying to get at what I think is
a very important point. The author of this manual is a white,
Anglo type, whose Norwegian grandparents, Minnesota upbringing
and seminary training (plus, no doubt, a lot of other things in the
genes and in the culture) conspired to inflate his estimation of
cerebral values and to diminish his appreciation of many more
fully human ones, to put it all too simply. I don't know quite
how to explain the human diminishment I have too recently
begun to feel—especially vis-a-vis black culture—except to say that,
in comparison with it, I feel ill-at-ease in my body, stiff, inflexible,
inhibited and somewhat constipated. Looking at problems of
liturgical celebration in congregations predominantly of "my type"
across this land, I do not believe I am unique or alone in suffering this kind of diminishment.

Here is where ethnicity becomes a rich resource, inviting learning and sharing, instead of an excuse for hostilities. These cultural groups—and, no doubt, many others—have so much to teach
and to share with the rest of us about these matters, when we
become free enough to learn. None of us can overcome native
cultural handicaps simply by wishing it were so, but we can become conscious of them and work to compensate for them (over-
coming in the process the fears and stereotypes by which we pro-
tect them), and practice until we no longer inflict them in extreme
ways upon other people.

The presider in liturgy has a very special need to become a
body person, at home in the flesh, moving gracefully and expres-
sively, gesturing spontaneously, saying something to people by
style in walking as well as in talking, communicating by the
rhythm and articulation of the whole person, knowing how to
dress up and wear clothing, etc. You can call it "soul," as many
do. Whatever you call it, our liturgical experience is in desperate
need of it. Because liturgy is play, ritual play, and play is something that worker-thinker types find difficult. Read Clarence
Rivers's *Soulful Worship* and NOBC's *Freeing the Spirit*. Experience Rivers's or Eddie Bonnemere's leadership in liturgical song,
or Jim Forbes's (formerly of Washington's Inter/Met, now of New
York's Union Seminary) preaching. Not to imitate, but to enter

a school of the whole person, a school of the body-attuned-to-the-spirit, to learn to feel . . . to learn to pop the cork and let those feelings seize the face, the hands, the arms, the legs, the torso, and take flesh.

The Presider's Preparation

Presiding in liturgy today requires considerable preparatory work, an expenditure of time and effort and money (budgets for celebration are new to many people). A real facing of the issue is apt to shock many of us clergy, unaccustomed as we are to this priority. Not only does the work of presiding now assume aptitudes and training formerly considered peripheral or tangential, but also that work taxes time and talent with the necessity of provisions and practice which go far beyond the homily and the general intercessions. The shock has registered already with some of us; not yet with others.

Ora et . . . labora

Even a limited acquaintance with the current parish scene suggests that the clergy who have been plugging for reform all along and who are well versed in the conversation and the jargon of renewal find it as difficult as anyone else to develop the skills and commit the time necessary to fulfill the role well. Collapse of the old depersonalized rigidity coupled with a defensive evasion of the new personal responsibilities has left countless parishes in a last state not much better than their first.

The presider who passes the test is the one who does the work. Sweet talk is easy, but the work is hard. Sweet talk may gain the presider a reputation as "with it," a "liberal," a "progressive," but what improves the celebrations of the faith community is the work that is done. The two previous sections of this manual have dealt also with the presider's preparation, but in a remote or long term sense. The spirit, definition of the role, attitudes of the first section are crucial and basic to everything that follows. The planning participation of the second is more immediate.

Here we turn to the immediate and frequently private preparation of the presider. And we must try to touch, at least, on all possibilities—those in parishes with a highly sophisticated and developed liturgy planning system and those whose group planning is less detailed and comprehensive. Clearly in the latter case, the presider's work is much more extensive, so it is necessary to mention some things here which the presider, ideally, should not be doing at all. Before we get into that, a brief review of some prerequisites for this immediate preparation is in order.

A mindset for the task

The person who is burdened with a clerical ecclesiology is doomed from the start, but the one whose ecclesiology is baptism and eucharist and covenant—a gathered community of sister and brother believers—is on a track that permits progress. The presider whose Christian identity is based on ordination is part of the problem. The presider whose Christian identity is solidly rooted in the faith community of the baptized is part of the solution.

One who leads in common prayer must be more than prayerful. By definition, any believer is a prayerful person, but there are different kinds of prayerfulness. Presiding in liturgy, because it is the common deed of the entire church, requires a kind of modest prayerfulness that is heavy on awe and mystery, light on answers and recipes. The one who frequently succumbs to the temptation to spell out God's will in lurid detail may be marvelous in a rally but is unsuited for the task of presiding in liturgy. This has something to do with liturgy's commonness. It has to do with vibrations which ring out self or God . . . with quite unequal results.

Together with this needed sense of awe and human limits, the presider must have some confidence in himself/herself. Leadership in worship as in anything else is a service to the community that flounders if one is unsure of one's training, understanding, efforts to "keep up," etc. We can recognize inadequacies and seek to correct them, but an underlying confidence is required to do even that. One need not have "all the answers" to be strong in this kind of leadership, strong in the conviction that one can function well in this role, strong in our efforts to improve.

And no faceless assembly can help us. Until that congregation appears to us as people with faces, personalities and names, we cannot really preside. A pastoral respect and reverence for people is an indispensable prerequisite. One sea of faces is very much like another, and the presider who sees only a sea of faces is the one whose manner will seem phony, distant, and preoccupied with self. But when one sees different faces, with different responses, different faces with different names and attitudes and needs (all with a claim on one who aspires to serve them), then the whole atmosphere is different and the vibrations are right.

A feeling for the movement and rhythm of ritual action is another requirement of a good approach to preparation. There is nothing terribly complicated about this sensitivity—one need only be aware of one's reactions (interest, attention, or the lag thereof) in any human social activity. The structures of the rites do not assume a long attention span. They are full of alternations between persons and groups of persons, between sounds and silences, between reading and singing, between rest and movement, between word and action, between light and darkness, between listening and other kinds of doing, and so on. If one takes a rite as a whole, there is a progression from gathering, to building up, to climax, to dismissal. Anyone who can take such rites and make them appear to be without form, rhythm or movement possesses a certain genius, to be sure, but it is not the genius of presiding.

Finally, among these mindset prerequisites, a word about words, about the poetic character of all liturgical texts. A society and culture that places a high value on accuracy of detail and the avoidance of figures of speech is going to have trouble with the verbal as well as the nonverbal language of liturgy. In liturgy we deal with things beyond our ken, with aspirations beyond our experience, with the givens of faith which strain our formulas at every point—in other words, we read and speak as symbolically as we act (notwithstanding the jingles that pass for lyrics in some of our music). This means a care with words, a striving for *paucity* of verbal expression in liturgy . . . and, when we do use words, an effort to make them really count. If we are aware that our words are poetic and symbolic, we may learn to be less heavy-handed with them, more delicate, more modest, more humble.

If we begin the discussion of the presider's immediate preparation for liturgy with the bare essentials, and if we accept the desirability of employing other ministers in addition to the presider in

Only the presider can . . .

any large group celebration, then what are the things that the presider absolutely must do? In any liturgy, the presider must serve by directing the course of the celebration, the ritual action, and by leading in that part of it which is its essence, its heart or center. In a eucharistic liturgy, for example, the presider conceivably could do only two things: 1) direct the entire celebration, while leaving to other ministers the overt leadership of all parts except the eucharistic prayer; 2) proclaim the eucharistic prayer (including, by implication, the ministering of holy communion). Ordinarily, of course, and quite properly, the presider does more than this, but here we begin with essentials.

The presider directs the entire celebration. If a master of ceremonies is employed in a complicated rite with many ministers, the master of ceremonies functions as an assistant to the presider, and an expediter, *not in place of the presider.* It is to the presider that all members of the congregation as well as all ministers have a right to look for guidance in the common action. That is why the presider should be visible to all at all times.

If the presider is looking at and listening to a reader, everyone knows that that is the thing to do. If the presider is sitting in quiet meditation, that is a signal for all. If the presider is addressing the assembly, we get ourselves together to listen and perhaps respond. If the presider raises a hand, we know we stand, or lowers a hand, we know we sit. An orchestra may know the music very well, but it still needs a conductor. The presider is the conductor of this orchestrated liturgy, this rite whose flow and parts can easily be shattered by the bark of needless orders and instructions: "Now stand!", "Now sit!", "Now turn to page 13!"

So the first obligation of the presider's immediate preparation is to get a firm handle on the celebration in question and all its parts: to know what will happen, when, by whom, how, and for what purpose. Some presiders affect a slightly dazed look, as if wondering what is coming next. Others wear that look quite honestly. Neither type should be permitted to go near a chair, altar, or lectern. The appearance of the person in that role is the most powerful signal the congregation has that the work it is engaged in has some importance, some meaning, some clarity and logic. A presider who looks baffled demoralizes an assembly without uttering a word, whereas one who is confident of the rite and its progression communicates positively with everyone.

When the service in question is a regular one, no special practice period with the other ministers may be needed. In that case, presumably, the ministers are accustomed to the action and accustomed to working together. This points up the advantage of having the same team of ministers (musicians, acolytes, ushers, readers and presider) at the same celebration regularly. Familiarity lubricates teamwork. When, however, the service is an unusual one, with special problems of logistics, movement, action, then such a practice is a necessity. And, since the presider's is the key role, no practice without the presider is very helpful.

Eucharistic prayer

In the case of the eucharistic liturgy, the other thing that the presider *must do* is the proclamation of the eucharistic prayer, together with the ministering of holy communion. Godfrey Diekmann, O.S.B. points out how early liturgical texts strongly link these two activities: the proclamation of the great prayer with the act of ministering the holy bread and cup. Phrases like "manu sua" (with the presider's *own hand*) show the urgency, even when the congregation is large enough to require auxiliary ministers, of the presider's continuing the action of the eucharistic prayer, confirming it and enfleshing it, in the personal gesture and contact of sharing the plate and cup, person to person.

Preparation for the eucharistic prayer can be a minor or a major task. Minimally, it involves the choice of a prayer from among options, gaining sufficient familiarity with it so that one need not keep one's eyes glued to the book, practicing broad gestures of prayer and sacrifice and invocation so that the body is proclaiming as much as the voice, learning how to look at people in a way that summons them to common prayer, and getting a feel for the rhythm between the proclaimed parts and the people's acclamations (so that there are no pauses between the presider's words and the congregation's song, either before or after).

Maximally, the preparation for the eucharistic prayer involves adaptations so that there is some interpretation of the covenant in terms of the people's current situation (what are the current faces and aspects of the graces of freedom and unity for which we give thanks?), and more attention to the congregation's participation through posture, gesture, and perhaps more frequently repeated acclamations. One can do this only with great sensitivity to the tradition—and to the elements which tradition establishes as essential in that prayer. Since it is both the key prayer and the key proclamation of the entire eucharistic liturgy, any adaptations should carefully preserve traditional elements and respect traditional texts.

Preparations for the eucharistic prayer—even minimal ones— can not ignore the most important thing of all: the bread and wine, the basic symbols with which we deal in the eucharist: bread to be broken and shared, wine to be poured out and shared. It seems to this writer that no single custom is as destructive of a fundamentally good eucharistic experience as the bread that is commonly in use among us: individually pre-punched, small, thin, tasteless, textureless, assembly-line wafers. Perhaps because pragmatic Americans are overawed by efficiency and convenience, this practice has somehow escaped critical scrutiny, even though it defies the elemental symbolism of the rite, the extremely significant fraction, and the General Instruction of the *Roman Missal.* Such "bread" lacks not only the baker's hand but also the taste, the texture, the smell, the shape and size of anything accepted as bread in our culture.

We shall return to this theme later in a discussion of the symbol language basic to all liturgy and our peculiar problem of opening up symbols which have been retained in a shriveled and petrified form. We can thank God for their retention during hard times, even while we lament the lack of attention to them over the last several centuries. Preparations for the eucharistic prayer which do not entail provision of real bread and wine, an effort to show one bread and one cup on the altar until the breaking of the bread, plates and cups for the altar and for communion which are impressively beautiful and noble works of human craft—preparations without those considerations are utterly inadequate and fail to honor the first principles of symbolic communication.

Preparation and spontaneity

Before getting into the other parts of liturgical celebration which require special immediate preparations by the presider, some reflections on the relation between careful preparation and spontaneity are in order. Such reflections are necessary because it is easy to fall into the trap of thinking that preparation and spontaneity are contradictory, or mutually exclusive. Quite obviously, some presiders and planners have already made that plunge.

To assume that the Holy Spirit assists only the totally unprepared is to give insufficient glory to God. We need not be that stingy. One of the contemporary scourges afflicting the liturgical celebrations of Christians is the pious hope (sometimes it seems a brazen assumption) that the random thoughts and expressions of presiders are worthy of universal attention. While this hope relieves the presider (who is only *one* of its victims) of much work, it is quite unfair to the church, which has a right to expect a liturgical celebration to be different from a parish council meeting. A totally impromptu spontaneity *is* contradictory to ritual action, and the only spontaneity which can aid ritual is the spontaneity enabled, nourished and disciplined by a strong and carefully prepared framework. Spontaneous elements are an important part of liturgy, but only a part. Without the programed, familiar elements of any ritual activity, spontaneity cannot have the character of public worship.

It is, therefore, precisely the careful preparation of all parts of the liturgical celebration, including and especially all of the presider's parts, which keeps the celebration on track, keeps the flow of words under control, and offers public worship a guarantee that spontaneity (when appropriate) will be helpful rather than hurtful. For example, the better prepared a homily is, the easier it is for the preacher to incorporate spontaneous reflections and the more relevant those reflections are apt to be.

The balance is difficult. It is easy to go with a "book liturgy," which no longer meets even the demands of the book or the rubrics, much less the needs of a living community. And it is also easy for some, apparently, to let the traditional structures of the rites dissolve into a sentimental, undifferentiated and clergy-dominated (even though the exact opposite is the intention) hullabaloo. Either undermines the liturgy and the liturgical experience of the people of God. Were this experience less important in the lives of believers, we could afford to be as unconcerned about the problem as many of us seem to be.

Spontaneity is not at all the same thing as adaptations. Adaptations are carefully worked out and prepared and are proper to the whole of liturgical celebration. They are programed into the already programed ritual structures and forms of the liturgical books. Spontaneity, on the other hand, cannot be programed. It can be only facilitated, encouraged and hoped for. Any specific service of public worship will reveal to the sensitive student of liturgy appropriate places for spontaneity. To list such possibilities at this time would be too restrictive, since we are only beginning to feel the need of some spontaneity, and since our initial attempts (as in general intercessions or dialogue homily) are tentative and exploratory.

Other elements to be prepared

Beyond the general direction of the entire ritual action and the active leadership of its central, essential, climactic element, it is customary and entirely appropriate for the presider to assume active leadership at a number of other points: 1) defining the beginning and end of the ritual action; 2) formulating or summing up the prayers (silent, vocal, or processional action) of the persons of the assembly; 3) preaching the word.

1) Defining the beginning and the end of liturgical celebration. There must be, of course, a clear definition of structure and parts throughout any service of public worship. Ordinarily this is taken care of by the content of texts, music, a variety of ministers, movement, environmental changes of focus, etc. It is especially important that the beginning (after music or a gathering song) and the end (before music or a departing song) are definite, ritually acceptable and understood by the assembly. The sign of the cross and a scriptural greeting by the presider fulfill this function admirably, for the beginning of any service; a spoken and gestured blessing and dismissal for the ending. Any adaptation (for example, a scriptural acclamation or versicle and response between the sign of the cross and the greeting) should have a heavily transcendent focus, inviting us all to face squarely the fact that this time and action is a special time and action. The substitution or addition of a "Good Morning" or "Hello" may at first seem hospitable, although the ushers should have taken care of that before this moment; in the end, it is merely disappointing. It deprives ritual action of a structural support it needs, *we* need.

2) Vocally formulating or summing up the prayers of the assembly. Traditionally a presidential function, this act of leader-

ship finds (in the eucharistic liturgy) its primary exercise in the eucharistic prayer, its secondary exercise in the opening prayer, the prayer at the conclusion of the general intercessions, the prayer over the gifts and the prayer after communion. The eucharistic prayer is briefly discussed above. Two of the three proper prayers (opening prayer and prayer after communion) are especially important as acts of pastoral leadership and definitions or turning points in the structure of the rite. The prayer over the gifts may seem a bit redundant in view of the eucharistic prayer which follows immediately, and a lesser item in view of the diminishing solemnity of the procession with gifts. And, while a concluding prayer does "tie up" the general intercessions, the latter could well at times stand on their own feet, both as prayerful reflections on the word with its homiletic exposition and as announcements of special intentions for which the sacrifice is being offered. The fact that some parishes announce "mass intentions" in a bulletin and pray for a series of quite different intentions in the general intercessions is testimony to our mental and spiritual confusion, and is damaging to the sacramental experience of the people.

The opening prayer is the conclusion of the entrance procession and the prayer after communion is the conclusion of the communion procession. The ending of the first and gathering movement leads to the proclamation of the word; the ending of the act of sharing in holy communion leads to the announcement of other activities of the faith community and then to a brief, succinct dismissal. These clear definitions of ritual structure should not be cluttered up with odd items—a good reason why the sprinkling should be used instead of the "penance rite" and why announcements following the prayer after communion, although important to affirm the church's mission, should be brief and to the point.

3) Preaching the word. This manual is not one of predictions for the future but one to be used in the celebration of Christians here and now. Persons who envision the eventual disappearance of the presider-as-homilist will have to defend their insights elsewhere. No matter how frequently we employ guest preachers or homilists from the congregation or dialogue techniques, at present

Preaching as clowning

the homily remains an ordinary part of the presider's task. There is even a certain cogency in this, for the coming together of the word of God with the realities of the human situation may be facilitated by (rather than handicapped by) a professional or full time clergy person, inasmuch as that person functions with respect to daily life and daily human roles and society as an outsider, a jester in the world's court, a fool, a critic.

Our need of this sort of person, this "outsider," is part of the reason for the clergy's existence. It is not that the worker or the executive or the craftsperson or the writer are incapable of preaching or should never preach. It is simply the real and inescapable fact that all of us are human, limited, finite creatures, and the professional clergy's freedom with respect to normal daily political and economic roles is not in all respects a disadvantage in holding those roles up to the light of the gospel.

Clergy who have worked hard at getting "inside" the political and economic arena and getting accepted will find this as puzzling as those in the Christian community who have concluded that the clerical function is passe. This manual disagrees with both and would like to see a generation of presiders who want to be fools, jesters, given to fantasy, who don't mind dressing up in crazy chasubles and doing unproductive things. The clown function in a social group is related to the critical function and also to the relieving function of one who helps everybody escape from social pressure for a moment.

Preparation for the homily, then, will be a major part of the presider's ordinary task. We hope The Liturgical Conference will publish a manual on preaching as a part of this ministries series, later on, because there is no way here to get into the prayer, the scripture study, the familiarity with the life of the community, and the skill of writing or outlining for oral discourse, which are all essential parts of homiletic preparation. The writing or the outlining of a homily is an exercise basically different from the act of writing something that is to be read. The preacher must be thinking speech and people's faces and an assembly's character as well as his/her own capacity for sharing the feelings elicited by the reflections. Literary rules are not for the writing or outlining of a homily. Hard as it is, for most of us, we should try to be thinking in this process of a congregation relaxed enough so that we can hear some of its members chanting "Right on!"

"Say it again!" "Amen," or uttering squeals of painful recognition.

In any case, the homily is part of a liturgy, so the principles of presiding discussed in these pages apply to the preaching function as well as to the other presidential activities: the body joined to the words, always; the eye contact and the reaching out; the immediate translation from the written to the oral; the loving tendering of one's person while one endeavors to minimize peculiarities and idiosyncracies. These are parts of a good liturgical style whether one is preaching or reading from a liturgical book. Other things being equal (admittedly, they usually aren't), the older person will be a better presider than the younger, because the job is elevating texts and ritual actions to the level of a sharing of experience. The greater a person's experience of the transcendent and the holy, theoretically, the better the presiding.

The immediate preparation of the presider may also (but will not always, when others have responsibility for these matters) involve considerations of art and environment and of action beyond that called for in the basic ritual structure. A large, well-organized parish will have persons in charge of altering and creating environments for celebration, at least for the major feasts and seasons. While the human community assembled is the most important liturgical reality in the environment, the shape and color and furnishings and decoration and arrangement of the liturgical space is also an important factor in the human experience of celebration. Even when no one seems to notice, these things have an influence on all of us that is as profound as it is subtle.

As with everything else in liturgy planning, when no one else has authority and responsibility for environment it is up to the presider to pay some attention to this powerful element (relying, of course, on the judgment of competent persons in art areas). The same can be said of gestures, actions, movements of ministers and congregation beyond those prescribed in the basic rite. An increasingly common recognition that we need to do much more in the area of body movement and gesture is one of the clear developments in these early years of reform and renewal.

The hesitancy we feel is partly cultural—at least for the white Anglo types among us—but it is also partly a legitimate fear of manipulating people and forcing a kind of ritual conformity which

Action and environment

is not genuine, not real. The problem here is that we are all one piece. "External" gestures are not merely the "outward" expressions of "inner" feelings—the human organism is more complicated than that. The reason for ritual action is that common movements and postures nourish and encourage good feelings just as much as feelings cause an expression in movement or posture.

Experience seems to indicate that initial resistance to the body's part in liturgical celebration is common, especially among middle class and upper class Anglo communities. However, experience also seems to indicate that when such groups become accustomed to more body movement and gesture they find these activities surprisingly rewarding and pleasant. Encouraging this is not so much a matter of manipulating people as it is of helping to break down some quite inhuman inhibitions.

So all of this amounts to an important and delicate pastoral question: how can we overcome prejudices among certain groups, or inhibitions, which effectively prevent the people involved from enjoying themselves in liturgical celebrations? One way, certainly, is for the ministers and leaders of celebration to do more in the way of movement, gesture, posture—encouraging the congregation but allowing them slowly to adapt. And, however we seek to involve people in these common ritual acts, we should encourage ourselves in the process with these pointed and profound remarks on the subject by William F. Lynch, S.J., in *Christ and Apollo: The Dimensions of the Literary Imagination* (New York: The New American Library, Mentor-Omega Books, 1963, p. 175; Sheed and Ward, 1960):

"Let me give a third example of a fact which, if reduced to but one level of existence, can produce the most disturbing repercussions in the human person. I am thinking of the instinctive drive in the soul toward ritual. This drive toward common movement and ritual existence is one of the most powerful movements in the soul of man. If it is choked off and denied on the deepest and religious levels of existence, as indeed it has been, it will concentrate the whole of itself on the most superficial levels of life, the immediately social, and will end in becoming an absolute, a parody of itself and of its own dignity. Whereas, if we were really united at the bedrock of our natures, most of the pressures toward the kind of conformism that all men really hate would be enormously lessened.

"The fact is that these pressures come from the inside of us and are not really being satisfied at the more vital points of the soul. Romantic rebellion is always the too obvious counterpole to the kind of cheap, overgrown ritualism which besieges us, but it is no solution; in fact it only intensifies the difficulty. The thought I have in mind . . . is that it has been the collapse of the idea of the church in our civilization that has driven us into our present social rites. Gimmick ritual has necessarily been substituted for the real thing . . . "

Whatever texts and rubrics are prepared and adapted for a celebration should be carefully contained within a handsomely bound large sacramentary or in another book of noble size and of rich binding. This is not to compete with the lectionary of scripture readings, which should have its own dignity and precious appearance. The other noble book is merely to recognize that this celebration is a formal liturgical action requiring some reading and an appropriate volume to read from, and that the liturgy demands the very best in human art and craft.

Preparation of implements

The spectacle of the presider (or any other minister) standing or sitting before the congregation with loose sheets of paper in hand, or with one of those little newsprint missalettes, is a more trenchant comment on the importance of what is happening in liturgy than any words which may be spoken. The test of any implement used in liturgy is its appropriateness and quality, in terms of manifesting the goodness, truth and beauty of God—not its convenience or its price.

Our American passion for convenience, for doing everything in the easiest and most effortless way, is one of our great liturgical handicaps. The essence of liturgy is that it is play, fantasizing the kingdom, doing apparently useless things with great solemnity, engaging in the excess which belongs to festivity. Using things not because they are appropriate and beautiful but because they are convenient is an assault upon the senses of people who have gathered for one of the grave and inspiring moments of their lives. They deserve to experience with the rest of their senses as well as with the ears the dignity and awesomeness as well as the hospitality and friendliness of the occasion.

Preparations for the celebration, then, should make sure that everything—books, vesture, furnishings, environmental art, symbols, vessels, in short each object that has any place at all in the liturgical action—is well made, beautiful, honest, noble, appropriate. Presiders will need the help and guidance of artists or art critics in this exercise of pastoral care.

Presiding in Liturgical Celebration: Environment

The principle that the assembly gathered for liturgy is the most important environmental factor should have been established in the earlier sections of this manual. It bears repeating, however, since nothing fruitful can be said or done about presiding style unless the presider is fully aware, fully conscious of that principle. If the focus of the presider's attention is on anything else—on style, or objects, or other symbols, or rubrics, or texts—there is no hiding that fact. It doesn't have to be articulated. The members of the congregation can feel it when they are not the primary focus of attention.

Far from having the effect of diminishing or reducing the other elements in celebration, this focus on people enhances all of them. When we realize clearly that our entire job in presiding is facilitating the assembly's *experience* of church, community of faith, kingdom witness, men and women together as sisters and brothers before God without the distinctions and roles and categories within which they operate daily—when that realization takes hold, then everything we do and say and handle and touch in liturgy, as well as the scene we set for the action, demands an attention that is greater rather than less. Now each element has to contribute to the experience of the people. Each element is not simply something that has to be done. It is something that has to be done because the doing of it is meeting real human needs.

Liturgy is the interaction of people in this assembly. A people focus, then, will begin with certain minimal conditions for this interaction. The first thing to be noted is that a theatre or auditorium is not and cannot be a model for the liturgical space. We have used them as such, consciously or unconsciously, for a long time. A far better model is the home. Everyone in the assembly must be capable not only of hearing and seeing easily with regard to the focal points of the ritual action to be done (for this the theatre and auditorium suffice), but also of seeing one another, corresponding with one another in common action, touching one another, joining easily in processions (e.g., communion), moving around for the peace greeting, etc.

Participation in song, response, common prayer, and other ritual actions is still a lonely matter when all one can see is the backs of heads and peripheral profiles. We need the life and encouragement of other people's eyes and expressions. We need to see them singing and speaking if we are really going to sing out and speak out. This is the kind of social atmosphere that elicits participation and sustains it. Not all the ministries in liturgy belong to leaders. The congregation has a ministry, too, and an important part in transforming the "audience" we have become into a community of actors. It is a real necessity, then, that persons in the congregation be able to see at least some of the other persons in the congregation, and to look in their faces, that we may revive one another.

And all must feel addressed, when the congregation is addressed. All must feel the water when the congregation is sprinkled. All must smell the scent and see the smoke, if the congregation is honored with incense. When there is greeting or bowing, no one should feel excluded by any mannerism or by any "efficiency" or paucity of gesture.

Hospitable atmosphere

On the basis of his study of the history of the architecture of church buildings, on the one hand, and the needs of contemporary celebration on the other (*Modern Architecture and Christian Celebration,* John Knox Press, 1968) Frederic Debuyst's recommendation of the home as the proper model for liturgical space concludes that hospitality must be a prime characteristic of that space and its assembly. Clearly, a concern for that quality involves the whole congregation, especially the ministry of ushers (as hosts), welcoming people, providing cloakrooms for their outer garments when necessary, introducing strangers to at least a few people in the congregation, providing them with any materials necessary for participation, seating them close together, and maintaining a warm and friendly atmosphere throughout the service.

An appropriate desire to make people feel at ease and at home seems to have spawned inappropriate conduct on the part of some presiders. A concern for hospitality need not be at odds with attitudes of reverence and a sense of mystery and awe in worship. Perhaps a feeling that these *are* somehow at odds has led some clergy to adopt a "style" of breezy familiarity that is not at all helpful. Reacting strongly to one kind of phoniness, it is possible to fall into another kind. Pretending intimacy in a gathering of a few hundred, or more, people is not much different from "marbelizing" a wooden altar. To say nothing of the fact that, as a large social event, liturgy requires a formality and choreography that would be inappropriate in a poker game or at an outdoor barbecue.

One does not help create a hospitable atmosphere for the celebration of public worship in ritual forms by being careless with those forms or indifferent to the people's need in ritual for the familiar and the practiced. One dare not forget that one is presiding in common prayer and needs both to have and to show the reverence and the feelings of awe and mystery which should be natural in the God-conscious. One must be aware that the liturgical moment is special and one must act in a special way. Being careless, vulgar, clumsy or unkempt is not being hospitable.

Hospitality requires style in its hosts and leaders (as well as in the members of the congregation), because it takes the assembly seriously. It recognizes that people must be comfortable and loose and at least somewhat free of the inhibitions and role-burdens of daily life in order to enter into the kingdom-play that is liturgical celebration.

A consequent sacredness

The sacredness of public worship does not derive from the place of worship, nor from the furnishings or objects used in worship. Sacredness derives from the Christian assembly and its liturgical action. It is the holiness of ecclesia in action that touches place, furniture, objects, and makes them special.

The looseness and comfortableness of hospitality, therefore, should be tempered by a strong group-consciousness, a desire to give oneself to an ecclesial action, to find oneself in relation to the other children of God. Liturgy is play, but play has rules, as we know from the games of both children and adults. Rules without which it cannot be play, because it is social.

Indicating the sacredness of the action with broad gestures of reverence and clear discipline of speech, posture, movement—these are not opposed to feelings of hospitality, but appropriate to the particular action in which the assembly is involved. Even the facial expressions of the good presider will have no trace of either self-centeredness or triviality about them.

The temptation to get carried away with feelings of this (derived) sacredness and consequently to begin to think of places, furnishings, objects as if they were more important than the people of the faith community on which they depend—that temptation is inescapable. It should not be resisted by treating place, furniture, objects with disdain or carelessness. Rather, it should be resisted by the constant conversion and purification of faith to which Christians are called.

Art and contemplation

Our environments for worship are as commonplace or even ugly as many of them are, not because we consciously prefer chaos to design and pretentiousness to authenticity, but because we do not really see them. The space—its form and color—and all the furnishings and objects within are necessities for the job to be done. As long as they are there, we get on with the job and we rarely stop to look at, to really see the places and the things we use.

We are Americans, pragmatic, efficient. We get things done. But the quality of life, the quality of what we get done and how we get it done—these questions embarrass us. They are diversionary tactics, in the view of many of us, which tend to complicate issues and create problems. In reality, of course, it is our efficiency and pragmatism that create problems for human life and human liturgical experience.

Until we take time to be contemplative, to stand back from things in order to see them better and let them speak to us, we will continue to form ourselves and our attitudes and feelings with fake and cheap and shoddy things. Until we begin to bring to the level of consciousness the formative power of environments (how different environments make us feel better or worse about ourselves and about what we are doing), we will not make the efforts that liturgy deserves and demands.

Unity of the space

If liturgy is the common action of an assembly or congregation served by several different kinds of ministers, then the first and overwhelming impression upon entering the liturgical space should be of its unity. It should be, clearly, one space, for one people and this one people's deed of common prayer.

A distinction of roles and a variety of roles are necessary to serve the action of the one assembly. When that distinction and variety obscure the unity, we have a problem, a situation that defies its own purpose. Overall the message and feeling of the space should speak solidarity. Then, within the one space, the spaces and furniture for particular congregational or ministerial functions are specified and arranged to facilitate celebration.

The entire assembly is holy. The entire assembly is ecclesia. So the functional arrangement of the one space is not dictated by a need to evidence status or rank. The various open spaces and pieces of furniture are arranged to make the exercise of different functions in the common action as smooth and clear and experiential for all as possible.

Seasonal environments

The more sensitive we become to the formative power of the physical environment—form, color, furnishings, visual emphases—the more we will want to modify the environment, sometimes extensively, for different feasts and seasons. The mere change of readings and other texts is not enough. Environmental alterations can create an Easter mood, a Pentecost mood, a Christmas mood, a Lent mood, or an Advent mood. Artists in the community can come up with ways of doing this that are rich, imaginative, subtle. Slogans-on-banners not only pale quickly but also fail to respect fully the peculiar character and materials of banners.

Presiders can contribute to the creation of special and seasonal environments by preaching and leading prayer with full awareness of and advertence to feast and season, by using vestments of appropriate colors, by encouraging liturgy planners to seek competence in art for the purpose of designing these environments and to introduce supplementary liturgical actions or gestures, when possible, which can illustrate or enhance the festal or seasonal emphasis.

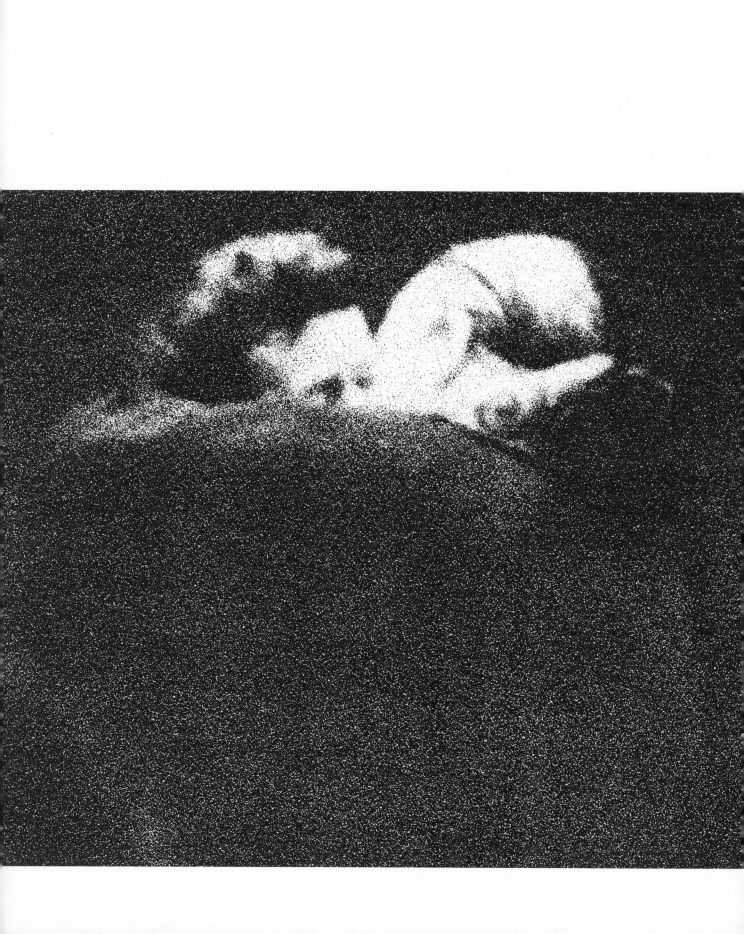

Presiding in Liturgical Celebration: Presence

Because the church is ministerial, the entire church is minister, and all specific ministerial functions depend on the church, a time of ecclesial rediscovery is also a time of ministerial rediscovery. All ministries, including those of bishops and presbyters, are undergoing a rethinking and reshaping, a radical critique. All this is essential, good, healthy for the churches as it is for the ministries. A manual on presiding can note these developments, as we have in earlier sections, but cannot give it the attention it must have. That attention depends on many essential studies now under way or in prospect.

The chair for presiding

It is not surprising that these developments should shake up the clergy and make the best of them—those most sensitive to the baptismal dignity of Christians and to the distance which now exists between ordained ministers and the rest of the church—uneasy in their presiding function. Perhaps the most important thing we can say in this manual is that it is not the function of presiding in liturgy that has created this distance, this inflation of the clergy and their separation from the churches. And it does not solve the problem to abdicate the presiding function.

One is tempted to sympathize with anyone who reacts against clericalism in any way, even if the reaction is clumsy, ill-considered and ineffectual. However, one should not sympathize with priests or other clergy who seem to think that refusing to preside is a contribution to the reformation of ministries.

The basic task in presiding has been described in the earlier section entitled "The Presider's Spirit." When a liturgical presider drops out of sight whenever the service does not require some vocal activity, or looks apologetic or ill at ease whenever it does, that person deprives everyone in the assembly of something that is essential to good liturgical experience.

Unlike a meeting of the Society of Friends, which has its own genius, sacramental liturgy requires specific ministerial functions, the most essential among them being the ministry of the congrega-

53

tion and the second most essential being that of the presider. Unless one is willing to accept the presider's role and do it as well as one can, one should not accept episcopal or presbyteral ordination.

One would think that Christianity's personalist faith would have less trouble with personal symbols, like the presider, than with static and thing symbols. This does not seem to be the case, however, and currently there is much show of diffidence and anxiety in any discussion of the presider's chair. People who miss the reserved sacrament's long and static reign over the eucharistic assembly are joined by prominent liturgiologists in worrying about the possibly doleful effects of the chair.

A chair in which the presider is neither lording it over nor distant from the rest of the assembly but present to it and in contact with it and in view of it and "chairing the meeting"—this, it seems to us, is not dispensable in liturgical celebration and it should not look disposable. It enables a function of service in a community gathered for a ritual that is the action of a community of persons and that requires a person to hold it all together. When that person also represents a collegial relationship with the other churches, it is a plus of considerable symbolic dimensions.

Naturally, if historical developments of one sort or another have alienated that person from the community and have infected that office with alien feelings, the chair may come to symbolize those feelings and that alienation. It is no accident that the chair has come back just as we begin seriously to attack the alienation, proving that the former is not the cause of the latter. The answer is not to get rid of liturgy (and chair) but to change the patterns of clerical recruitment, training and life that have caused the alienation.

Meanwhile, a liturgical celebration needs a presider who is present to, visible to, in touch with the entire assembly at all times in the course of a service of public worship. That person is the assembly's servant as well as the servant of any other ministers required by the particular rite. One's service, in this case, is not a question of self assertion but of leadership. To abdicate this leadership is to fail to serve the community.

Personal attention

Physical presence is only the beginning of a presence, but it is a sine qua non. The presider must be present to the assembly as a warm body—that's why the chair is important even when the presider is not actively leading at a particular moment. But liturgical presence that remains merely spatial is disastrous, as all Christians know from experience.

Personal attention throughout the celebration is one of the primary characteristics of a good presence. This means at the very least that one is "together," and is trying to stay together. The constitutive elements of this personal attention are probably many and complex, but it is certain that one cannot manifest it unless one feels that what one is doing is worth doing.

Personal attention

Faith is involved fundamentally, and an extraordinary conviction about the centrality of liturgy in the life of faith, a conviction about the moments of celebration as faith-life orientation. Unless one has discovered a necessary relation between faith and happiness in one's own life, it cannot be reflected or communicated. And if liturgy is felt (no matter how subconsciously) to be a packaged talisman, a thing, rather than a community's praising action, one's presiding will do more harm than good.

Personal attention in the whole and in each part of celebration is, like all the other elements of presence, communicated by the voice, the eyes, facial expressions, gestures, body postures and movements, the way one handles material objects, and so on. Specifics will be discussed below, under "Style," but the feeling that the presider is together and is attending to the persons of the assembly, the ritual action and the objects employed in it is a critical ingredient of a good experience for all.

Personal peace

Separation and distinction of these elements is a theoretical exercise, because they all go together, but it is necessary in a manual of this sort. If the presider is together and capable of focusing attention, he/she also needs a peace that comes, not from an absence of the doubting that always accompanies faith, but from facing doubts and reaching a daily resolution and commitment.

No doubt it is very honest and open and vulnerable and all those good things to stand before a congregation week after week testifying to one's anguish and uncertainty. It is also extremely inappropriate in liturgy and an abject failure in service or ministry. One's presence, then, becomes a burden on the assembly rather than a facilitating leadership.

We cannot ask less of the presider than we ask of other members of the faith community. Now that our baptismal consciousness has been raised a bit (or is in the process of being raised) and we see Lent and Easter as an annual reinitiation and recommitment for all Christians, we are beginning to realize that a personal commitment is our entry to the eucharistic assembly. The presider's commitment is of the essence. When no commitment can be summoned—and this can happen to clergy as well as to anybody else—the church should remain supportive and encouraging to that person, but its liturgies should not be made victims. A stiff upper lip is insufficient for the presider's task.

Personal peace is not apathy nor is it comfort in a rut. It is an active resolution of real human conflicts. It belongs to life, not to death. It is a work of struggle, not a yielding to rest. And what a service it is to an assembly of struggling believers, who bear daily in their bodies, the world-kingdom tension, the cross! It is a presence that everyone can feel.

Being onself

At one time—a time this author remembers well—it was popularly considered desirable for the one presiding to be as anonymous as possible. The less of oneself that showed through, the better. The ideal was pretty much an obliteration of self in liturgical celebration, if that isn't putting it too crudely.

As is true of so many other ecclesiastical precepts, the fact that this rarely happened in practice did not daunt the zeal of its proponents. One can even understand how we got that way. In those days, every detail of text, gesture, movement was rigorously specified. The "liminality" of liturgy was evident on a much more superficial level (language and rubrics) than the one on which we now base its "threshold" and kingdom fantasy character. Undoubtedly, that is one reason why some anthropologists like the "old" liturgy so much better than the "new."

The trouble with that effort (to be other than oneself) is its futility and costliness. We can't escape ourselves at any time, especially when we are exercising a function of leadership. Only the one who recognizes the futility of the effort to be anonymous and is without illusions will be effective in minimizing individual idiosyncracies and peculiarities for the sake of the social event. And the costliness of anonymity is a matter of experience: the "sacred alias" that was responsible for so many past and present problems, e.g., "pulpit tone," mechanical performance, failure to summon one's talents, and other manifestations of phony or unreal behavior.

Part of one's service to the assembly as presider is to be willing to present oneself to the whole group, consenting to be a focal point in the action, being in constant communication with the other ministers and the entire assembly through eye contact, gesture, body posture and movement, as well as word. The self-centered person, the ecclesiastical prince, the person who is out for privileges and status is opaque in this role. If, however, the presider is close to and part of the lives of all in the faith community, one of the people, clearly the servant of all, then there is the possibility of being transparent to the presence and action of the Lord. But it is a transparency that is accomplished, not with an anonymous persona, but with oneself.

Liturgy is something that persons of faith do in community. And they have to bring their real selves and their whole selves and their true selves to it. Surely they step out on the "threshold" of their daily lives and roles and categories to play at being sisters and brothers, daughters and sons of God—stripped of everything enslaving or divisive—but they can do this only as themselves.

So, when one functions as a presider or other minister, it is the whole person, the real person, the true person, the full and complete person who functions. It is you the church has chosen for this task. It is you God calls through the church. God wants no sacred alias, no pulpit tone, nor does the church.

Of course the personal nature of the presider's presence was always evident in liturgy, but more as a reluctant concession to humanity than as a desirable and valuable gift. Now we see it positively as a gift, a gift to be disciplined by the social and formal and ritual nature of the occasion, but a gift nonetheless.

The other ministers

To preside is to work with and facilitate and direct or conduct not only a congregation's action but also a number of other ministers: choral and instrumental musicians, readers, ushers, acolytes and others. One's service to the other ministers is chiefly to facilitate a team-making process, by attending to the value and the specific contribution of each and by choreographing or orchestrating their ritual interaction.

Working with the same team of other ministers week after week is very helpful to the presider's growth and performance. One must balance this value with the desirability of opening ministries to as many as possible in the faith community who have talent, training and desire for them. In most places, it should be possible to have a presider working with the same team of ministers for at least a month or a season at a time.

This practice enables members of the team to become sensitive to one another's unspoken cues, to move together more easily, to give full attention to the one or more of their number who are actively functioning at any given moment. The presider thus learns to conduct the group by simple glances and gestures, rather than by agitated whispers and scurrying about. The presider's presence to the other ministers is their focus and stable point of reference throughout the action.

Efficiency versus liturgy

Few things threaten one's effectiveness as a presider and the presence one has to establish as much as the lust for efficiency. Preceding pages have spoken of the importance of art, beauty, contemplation in celebration, and have described the play character of liturgy. But the work ethic and a compulsion to get things done as quickly, cheaply and with as little inconvenience as possible is never far below the surface in American church life.

This is not simply a matter of style, though it enters into every aspect of one's style. The whole presence of the presider is affected by one's approach to the words as well as to the action. If what counts for a person is getting the words said with the least expenditure of energy, that comes through as a negative experience for everyone in the assembly. If what counts is getting the actions performed with the least expenditure of energy, that, too, comes through as a totally negative experience.

Better use ten words and treat them lovingly and speak them meaningfully and savor them tenderly than ratatat a thousand. Better use one gesture and make it a real picture, make it big and broad and smooth, than try to signify anything with a hundred muscular spasms. Do not hurry. Do not abbreviate. Do not shortchange. Do not condense. Do not telescope. Do not "reduce to essentials" in the sense of "getting everything in" no matter what the cost or speed.

The usual excuse for this elephant-in-a-china-shop approach to rites is time. Many Christians, as a matter of fact, *are* time conscious during liturgical celebrations . . . because they are having a bad experience. If people are having a good experience, they stop looking at their watches, they have no interest in their watches. It does not occur to people who are having a good experience to wonder about the time.

But the presence of a presider who is conscious of time and unconscious of the value of the persons and things dealt with in the ritual action is enough to glue anybody's eyes to the second hand. Such a one communicates impatience and haste and lack of concern as the carrier of a contagious disease spreads its malevolence.

Keeping things together

The presider's physical presence is an elementary sign to all in the assembly that the liturgical action is one thing, one ritual, with a beginning, a middle and an end. Even if there is general movement during the course of a rite from one place to another (e.g., when there is a procession, or when the congregation moves from a place with seats for the proclamation of the word to an open space with altar for the rest of the eucharist), the visible presidency of the same person is a unifying element.

When the presider looks the part, looks as if he/she knows quite well what is coming next, chairs the action and facilitates the ministries involved with an easy assurance, then the togetherness and smoothness of the whole rite can be experienced by all. This depends to a great extent on the presider's participation in planning and on the presider's preparation, both of which were discussed earlier in this manual.

On the other hand, when a presider looks confused, baffled, uncertain about what to do, this extremely unsatisfying feeling spreads throughout the assembly. We have all seen—and we know how difficult it makes any real participation—the helpless presider, reaching out for a master of ceremonies as for a Seeing Eye dog, perplexed by the movement of a ritual action which clearly has escaped control.

Or we have seen the anxious whispered conversations with other ministers, or the paging about in a ritual volume whose pages should have been marked before the service began, or sudden disappearances into the sacristy for items that should be on the credence table. If these problems sound "picky" to those whose absolute confidence that "externals" do not matter is unaffected by their experience, please stop and think how all of these things have profound psychological as well as logistical effects on a celebration.

Keeping things moving

Any liturgy or ritual action is a composition of parts of great variety: song, speech, silence; proclamation, reflection; programed events, spontaneous participation; word, deed; movement, stillness; actions of different ministers, corporate actions of a congregation; preparation, building up, climax and dismissal. If these parts appear disjointed, do not flow into and out of each other smoothly, are not orchestrated by a conductor, they simply do not function. They look like an accidental juxtaposition of unrelated things.

A good presider will keep them moving, accenting the more important elements, playing down the less important, with a hand always on the thread of prayer and praise and purpose that runs through the whole service, making sure that transitions from one part to another are appropriately defined, clear, calm, and unsurprising.

In the eucharist, for example, when a congregation has become sufficiently attuned to and comfortable with the action, there may be a tendency to overextend a dialogue after the homily or the general intercessions with too many spontaneous contributions, or to make the ritual exchange of peace into a social hour of chit-chat, or to inflate the announcements at the end of the liturgy, before the dismissal, into a series of speeches on pertinent problems of the day. The presider should see to it that these sorts of abuses, which obscure the relations of the different parts of the liturgy and the transitions between parts, do not occur. This is done, of course, not by barking military orders but by using music, the offices of ministers, and the presider's symbolic gavel (an announcement that recalls the purpose of the rite) in a pastoral and friendly way.

Part of the presider's skill in keeping things moving is to sufficiently anticipate when a certain object will be needed, so that a discreet signal can be given to the appropriate minister in time to have it fetched and available as needed. To wait until the previous part of the service has been completed and an unscheduled silence reigns before one begins to look around for a book or a sprinkler or a censer or a cruet (or whatever) is to exhibit insufficient skill for the job. Protracted silences are an important part of liturgy, but these should occur as integral parts of the rite, not as accidents of unpreparedness. The difference is obvious.

If the presider has participated in planning the celebration and if the preparation homework has been done, then the sequence of the service will be etched in the mind and one will be able to do the conducting and the moving-on required.

Presiding in Liturgical Celebration: Style

Musing about death, Samuel Beckett wrote: "I shall be natural at last." It is a devastating illustration of the mental illness of our culture that we are apt to think of style as something unnatural. Pledged by the fabric of our social life to a "life is real, life is earnest" view of the human person as worker or as thinker, we find any diversion from the production of objects or ideas a waste of time and (therefore) money.

It is part of the contemplation problem mentioned earlier in this book. To slow down (and stop "producing") long enough to look at a person's mode or manner of acting—dressing, walking, dancing, loving, eating, presiding—or at the environments in which these things are done is difficult for most of us. Getting things done seems more important. So we minimize or lose much of the beauty and pleasure of life, in which our manners and our style communicate, more deeply and more honestly than anything that we can say, what we feel about ourselves, what we feel about other persons, what we feel about the objects and the things we use and deal with.

Good style in liturgy is the opposite of what is "put on" or "phony." Good style is appropriate, honest, authentic, as real and genuine as it can be. Good style means that we like ourselves and like other people. Good style is a result of understanding that means and ends are not as distinct as we sometimes suppose, flow into and out of one another, are related—and that means are so important that perhaps every step along the way is worthy of as much attention as the goal. Good style is acting consciously and humanly and with grace in every living moment.

Liturgy heightens the importance of style, because of its uniqueness as a human activity. In the liturgical assembly we are striving to be at the height of our God-consciousness and therefore at the height of our human-consciousness. It is an awesome thing to face the mystery of the Other and the mystery of ourselves with such clear purpose and intent. The obvious inadequacy of words and language in this enterprise makes our worship rest (even more heavily than other events do) on symbols and on style.

Style is like politics, in that neutrality is an illusion or a euphemism. When one acts in any capacity, there is no such thing as a neutral style. When people or churches say they are neutral in politics, they mean they are solidly behind the status quo, whatever that happens to be. So, when a presider claims to have no interest in such a trivial matter as style, she/he reveals a smugness and a satisfaction with the way things are. Meanwhile, the presider's manners and ways of doing the job affect everyone in the assembly, every time it gathers, for better or for worse.

For the presider to work on style, then, is simply to recognize the truth of the situation, to respond to the needs of the situation with art and with care, to take the job seriously enough to really try to get good at it. In this manual attention is on the presider, but style is also a responsibility of the other ministers and of the congregation. All together create the atmosphere, the mood, the experience of liturgical celebration. It remains true, however, that no one in the process is more influential than the presider.

Contrasting styles

When Leonard Bernstein's "Mass: a Theatre Piece for Singers, Players and Dancers" opened the John F. Kennedy Center for the Performing Arts in Washington, D.C. in 1971, two clergymen interviewed on television opined that the composer had "failed" because he "didn't understand Catholic liturgy." Bernstein's work, of course, was not supposed to be a musical setting for Christian liturgy. It was a theatre piece, as it was titled. And the interviewees were people of travel and experience. They had participated in liturgies in lots of places.

They saw, as this author did, the way that Bernstein handled the reading of God's word. An instrumental interlude ending with a crescendo preceded the reading. As the crescendo passage began, two ministers walked slowly from the wings through the crowd of people on the stage to the central figure clothed in presiding vesture. One of the ministers carried a huge, handsomely-bound book, perhaps 26 by 18 inches. The other carried a smoking censer.

When they reached the priest-figure, they stood facing him.
He acknowledged them, opened the great book with marked
deliberateness, and let his hand rest upon it while the minister
held it for the reading. The music reached its climax, ceased
into a moment of anticipatory silence, and then the "celebrant"
began to read. He read in a loud, slow, clear, appropriately in-
flected voice, not perfunctorily but savoring the words and
letting them ring out. The reading was followed by a simple
but haunting melody and song: "You cannot imprison the word
of the Lord."

One wonders where the clergy whose pronouncement flashed
across the country after the first performance celebrated the
eucharist on the following Sunday. This author assisted at mass
in a Washington parish well known for its exceptional liturgical
efforts. The congregation had scarcely finished a muttered
"Thanks be to God" after the second reading, when the reader
continued rapidly: "Please-join-in-the-Alleluia-on-page-ten-Alleluia-
Alleluia-Alleluia."

After she, like Bob and Ray, had said her song, the congregation repeated, dully and without music, "Alleluia-Alleluia-Alleluia."
The reader retired. The presiding priest shifted forward a foot
or two from his chair, held up one of those little newsprint missalettes, and, without any ceremony at all, read the gospel as if he
had already done it several times that day.

The contrast between the two experiences was striking. If one
had not got the true word from the TV interviewees, one would
have been tempted to say that Bernstein's theatre piece grasped
what Catholic liturgy is about, while those who were actually
doing it in a parish didn't seem to have the faintest idea. In the
theatre piece, everything that was done was done in earnest, with
a respect and care that were visible and tangible in gestures and
in movements and in the quality of all the materials employed.
The audience there could not help but become involved, because
everyone the audience could see on the stage was totally *into*
this thing. In the actual mass, everyone seemed to be absent.

This is why we talk about style, then. Because the clergy are
servants, and because our service in the critical area of liturgical
celebration has been, if not a minus in the life of the faith community, at least not a very noticeable plus. Yet the Sunday
eucharist is where the faith community gets itself together, real-

izes itself as church. What a difference we could make, if we chose and labored and strove to do so.

A sense of human limits

The "atmosphere of hospitality," stressed above as an essential and basic characteristic of a good liturgical environment and experience, should not be misunderstood. It means that everything possible must be done to help people feel "relaxed," "at home," physically comfortable and comfortable with each other, so that the assembly's celebration, its common prayer and praise and ritual action is uninhibited by feelings of isolation, alienation, estrangement, fear, suspicion.

However, the hospitality of the liturgical assembly is sui generis. Ordinarily human hospitality is offered by a host, with the host's property and goods. A sensitive—especially sensitive—host may act in a manner that reflects awareness of the fact that all property, all goods are God's. But there can be and is a vast range of degrees of this awareness. In the liturgical assembly, where we enjoy the hospitality, property and goods of a faith community *as faith community*, the awareness that everything is God's has to be intensely clear and overt. Even the slightest suggestion of a proprietary attitude on the part of the presider or any of the other ministers and servants of the congregation is a liturgical disaster.

It is not difficult to understand how some clergy develop proprietary attitudes and expressions. In fact, it is relatively easy for a pastor to do so, precisely because of the clericalist traditions from which we are now trying to extricate ourselves. The relevant point here is that when one succumbs to that temptation, it is immediately and grievously evident in one's style. The other members of the faith community soon begin to feel that they are guests in the pastor's house rather than at home in their own. (And that is only one of a million little visceral tricks we have for frustrating ecclesial renewal.)

Before discussing the primacy of reverence in the presider's style, we must first have a clear sense of human limits, creatureliness, well established in our guts. People in love with their property always tend to be painful. But a clergyperson who treats the place or act of Christian liturgical assembly as a private acquisition, a boast, a success story is unspeakable. Like the rest of the church, the pastor has to be struck to the roots of his/her soul by the unimaginable liberty of prayer, the grace of forgiveness, the awesomeness of faith. On a more mundane level and practically speaking, it is not the pastor who "lets" the congregation in. It is the entire congregation, the church, the faith community which "lets" one of their number, ordained for this purpose, preside.

Along with this sense of human limits, a feeling and attitude of reverence, a sense of mystery and of the fact that the action in which the assembly is engaging is a mystery—this feeling and sense is indispensable and inimitable. In the recesses of one's heart, as a person of faith, every presider possesses this, but in those recesses it does not help the assembly as much as it can if it is enfleshed and embodied. People must be enabled to experience in the presider's posture, gestures, movements, words this intangible and essential feeling. In different cultural situations, reverence may have different expressions, but it is communicable and it is communicated. It is the faith-sense of the people being the whole Christ, of church as the body of the Lord.

Reverence and sense of mystery

There is no conflict between reverence/sense of awe, on the one hand, and the atmosphere of hospitality, on the other. Reverence is not stiffness and pomposity—quite the opposite, for those qualities involve a self-assertion and a feeling of self-importance that are antithetical to reverence. What is less apparent is the psychological fact that efforts to make people feel at ease in liturgy, unless they are built upon and suffused with this sense of mystery, cause people to recoil rather than to relax.

In liturgy, the numinous, the holy must be almost tangible. It must be evident in the presider's attitude toward the other persons in the assembly, as well as in everyone's attitude toward everyone else. If we do not feel in liturgy that there is more to us than meets the eye, that we are dwelling places of the Most High, that beneath our masks and roles and camouflage and superficial categories we share a common dignity as well as a common creatureliness, then one of the more important functions of liturgy and ritual experience is unfulfilled.

Holy must be tangible

Liturgy is a kingdom scene, where people are supposed to be naked, stripped of their daily burdens and statuses (even of their sex and color), and the only thing that can make tolerable such a surrender of our defences is a palpable corporate consciousness of God. Before God, we are sisters and brothers only, and if we cannot find, or lose, the sense of mystery and reverence we are thrown back on our clothes or class or work, back into a relatively trivial situation which cannot support common prayer.

The numinous must be palpable, too, in the way the presider (and all) treat the symbols and the objects used in worship. To try to wean people from possibly superstitious attitudes to objects by treating the objects casually, or even carelessly, is both wrong and seriously harmful to the persons involved. Clumsy efforts like this are perhaps responsible for the reactions of many so-called "traditionalists" and others who have seized upon Latin or some other preconciliar custom to focus and express their appeal for a sense of the holy.

The ability to communicate this sense is nourished at the same time the presider nourishes an inner life of faith and prayer, although the former does not always proceed from the latter. The presider needs both to experience faith and prayer as personal needs and to take symbols and sacraments seriously. When a person of deep faith and prayer does not reflect in liturgical celebration the reverence the assembly needs, it may be because the liturgical deed is regarded subconsciously as a largely irrelevant formality. The gnawing human need for ritual and symbolic expression is foreign to such a person's thought. It cannot be permitted to remain so.

Enthusiasm and success

It is dangerous to discuss this quality, because anyone who has lived very long is suspicious of enthusiasms. We know how they come and go. We know how they are, so very often, wasted on trivial activities and causes. But we also know how powerful enthusiasm is, and how the presence or absence of it is frequently the difference between a leader and a person who merely occupies the limelight. Several years ago, a *Washington Post* reviewer concluded his remarks about a book called *The Happy Hooker* with this sentence: "It just goes to show how important enthusiasm can be to success in one's chosen profession."

The devil doesn't have to have all the laughs or all the good lines . . . or all the enthusiasm. Most presiders have made the work of the church their life work. A flame existed once, and even if the embers are now quiet they can be revived. The regularity (by definition) of ritual and liturgical celebration suggests that, if enthusiasm is required for good presiding style, it cannot be totally dependent on glands and body chemistry.

A good presiding style, as a matter of fact, does require enthusiasm—in the sense of a palpable commitment to the human need for church and, therefore, for those liturgical celebrations which constitute church. Almost every aspect of style is a facet of the same reality and commitment, but there is a point in focusing attention on the facets. Like the liturgical year, which feeds the paschal mystery to us in pieces small enough to chew, the facets are avenues of growth in and penetration of the mystery.

When the emotions associated with enthusiasm are dry, as they are sometimes in everyone's experience, the quality of this commitment survives to meet the dictionary definition: "an absorbing or controlling possession of the mind . . . " (Like the "personal attention" discussed in the section on "Presence" above.)

Person-to-group

The presider must be conscious of and conscious to every person in the assembly and every part of the assembly. This is why we have placed what some might consider an undue emphasis on the presider's accessibility and visibility and audibility and immediacy throughout any liturgical action. Part of the structural thread that ties the action together from beginning to end, the presider functions as a personal thread, even when neither vocal nor mobile.

A neglect of any part of the assembly or of any minister or group of ministers (e.g., musicians) may be blatant in an action like the incensing or the sprinkling or the peace greeting, but it can be sensed in other and less obvious parts of the liturgy as well. If the presider is conscious of everyone, then that consciousness will be evident in so many ways that no one will be able to mistake it: in glances, gestures, the leading of prayer, the handling of objects.

Darting glances to one bench or section of the assembly, as if to establish contact with the whole, is not helpful. One must train one's gaze to move about and take in all. Nor is the handling of an object so that one part of the assembly has a view of it any more than a needless reminder to the others that they are on the outside. When the congregation is on three sides of the altar area, as in most new or renovated buildings, this means taking time with gestures and with movements and with objects, so that everyone is included. For example, when the candidate is immersed in baptism, or when bread and wine are handled, broken, poured in the eucharist, these basic, elementary ritual gestures should be missed by no one. They must be brought very close to everyone. More below on this, in "Opening up the symbols."

When there is a processional entrance at the beginning of a liturgy, the procession should move as much as possible through the entire congregation. When the congregation is part of the processional movement, it will enter the liturgical space before the presiding minister and the other principal ministers, so that the ministers are identified with it and emerge from it in order to serve it.

Another part of the person-group rapport is assurance that participation aids (e.g., singing practice, singing and responsory materials) are available to everyone. This non-exclusion is even more important when the issue is a symbolic object which the members of the congregation use or receive in the course of a rite (e.g., holy communion, ashes, branches, candles).

Person-to-person

Within the communal celebrations of sacraments or other rites, the presider relates not only to the congregation as a whole but also, at certain moments, to individuals as individuals. Perhaps the distinction is not necessary, but experience suggests that it is. Rapport with a group as group is not the same as rapport with individuals in a group, with individual members of a group. One may have a certain group style yet fail to show respect for the other ministers or fail to give undivided attention to individuals in moments when that is appropriate. Moments of direct, person-to-person confrontation are among the most precious in any liturgy.

Since the eucharist is, at this time, the most frequent and ordinary liturgical experience for many Christians, it makes sense to illustrate this point with the example of sharing holy communion. No matter how many assistant ministers of communion may be needed or employed, the presider will always minister the sacrament to at least a portion of the congregation. What is said of this act can be applied to every other person-to-person moment in public worship (baptism, laying on hands, anointing, presenting an object, etc.).

In this particular act, it might better visualize the ministries as service if, instead of receiving *before* the congregation, the presider and all other ministers gathered around the altar *after* ministering to the congregation. There the presider could minister the holy bread and cup to each of the other ministers and be the last to receive.

Ministers receive after everyone else

When in the act of ministering communion, the communicant stands before the minister of the plate and then before the minister of the cup only for a moment. That moment offers an opportunity for a locking of the eyes and a touching of the hands in respectful attention and mutual encouragement—i.e., in recognition of the meaning of this sacrament of peace and unity. The presider looks at the communicant and the communicant looks at the presider. One does not expect a grin or a grimace. One does expect, and one has a right to expect, a look of respect and reverence, of care and communion. If one can speak here of electric current without any sexual connotation, it is such a moment.

Some of the problems of style are indicated by the fact that such a simple experience as sharing in holy communion impinges on and affects the human person in a great number of ways. It is an experience of the individual not in opposition to the collective but as attaining a new height both as person and as member. It is an experience of dance, of a sort, in the processional movement. It is obviously a gustatory experience. It is a visual experience of interrelation with the minister of the plate and the minister of the cup.

It is also an experience of touch. Where the holy bread is received in the hand, the communicant holds out both hands, palms up, one hand resting upon the other. The minister touches the palm of the hand as the bread is placed upon it, with words like "Sister (Maria), the body of Christ" and her answering "Amen." Again, the minister of the cup and the communicant lock eyes and exchange a touch as the cup is passed into the communicant's hands and then received back (for the rim to be wiped with a cloth before the next sharer sips).

71

Time has little to do with the intensity of an experience. Much can happen in this moment, if style is attended to and every aspect is treated with care and concern. Dormant feelings of faith and hope and love can be revived, if this moment is grasped, if the presider and the other ministers appreciate the importance of the moment and the right of every member of that assembly to its full value.

The personal contact and interaction between minister and communicant is extremely important in this rite as elsewhere. All of this is lost when either plate or cup is simply placed upon the altar to be approached by each communicant, without the hands of the other party, the minister. Yet one sees this practice—especially with reference to the cup—in many places, often initiated with the desire to improve participation. It should at least make us more cautious in considering *all* the effects of any proposed "reform."

Intinction is another practice which seems to this author to impoverish the communion rite, although one must admit its ingenuity. Who would have thought that anyone could devise a method of celebrating a sacrament of eating and drinking that practically bypasses *both* activities?

Searching the memory can help improve the style. At least, if you remember as this author does a number past counting of hurried and harried and distracted presiders (distance may magnify their stylistic defects), with chasubles flying, with eyes for everyone but the communicant. They might have been checking the lines of the communion procession. They might have been checking the other ministers. They might have been checking the quantities needed for plate or cup. They might even have been checking their grocery list. At any rate, they whisked by, speaking words apparently intended only for their own reassurance. One feels the loss now more than one did then. One hopes they do, too.

Opening up the symbols

At almost every one of these subheadings, the temptation is real to add an exclamation mark and say, "Now *this* is the most important one of all . . . " But they all go together and they are all important to presiders who want to be good servants, who want to do an honest day's work for an honest day's pay. (The problem of pay, of course, is another problem for another book, but it is not at all unrelated to style. In fact, there is a certain futility hanging like a cloud about this manual—as well as over most of what we are saying today about eucharistic celebration—as long as many clergy depend heavily on gratuities such as stipends. Money is one symbol that has lost none of its punch and meaning.)

Given the pragmatism, efficiency, technology and literalism of the culture we absorb and breathe and live, the problem which liturgy as a language of symbols presents to us is overwhelming. Whether our spiritual home is in the Catholic tradition or in the Reformed, we have real problems with symbols and with symbolic communication. The roots of the problems may be somewhat different, but the plants and the flowers are remarkably alike.

In the case of Catholic tradition, there has been a nominal adherence to traditional symbols and symbolic gestures, because they were frozen at a given time in the rubrics and texts of the rites. They were retained in this static, shriveled, desiccated form, which happily kept a shred of evidence for more perceptive times but which was considered supernaturally potent without the necessity of signifying, at least in any broad, full, sensory way.

On the other hand, the Reformed tradition abandoned many of those already-diminished symbols on its flight to the shrine of the printed word. The latter, after several centuries of monopolistic control over Reformed public worship, is ready to admit its limitations and team up with a multi-leveled sensory and ritual approach.

Capsule descriptions like the above are severely limited, but they have the truth of caricature. Like Western culture generally, both situations are symbolically impoverished and in need. That culture encouraged one of the first, and certainly one of the most ill-considered pastoral reflex actions during the decade after the Second Vatican Council in many churches of Catholic tradition: the abandonment of many (admittedly petrified) symbols and symbolic gestures, much as had happened among the Reformed centuries earlier.

This did not happen because of anything the Council or post-conciliar documents said, but because of clergy and liturgy committees who were victims of a long book-liturgy tradition and who consequently asked the new vernacular texts to bear the whole burden of celebration.

They tended to equate symbols and symbolic gestures with a quasimagical approach to sacraments and public worship, an approach that sees sacraments only as efficacious causes. After all, the symbols and symbolic gestures had been retained for so very long in desiccated forms, mere shadows of their former selves. Who would have thought that it might be wise to try opening them up and using them broadly and fully and letting them speak to us all again in their own inimitable way (without having to bear the additional burden of our "explanations")? The sacraments cause because they signify, and therefore they depend as much upon the communicative power of symbol and gesture as they do upon that of the word, but that fact escaped our pragmatic and no-nonsense approach to life.

It was easier for many just to talk a lot . . . a *lot*. And the more we multiplied our words and chatter in the liturgy, the weaker and more impotent every word became. Now we need to face the fact that it is care for opening up the symbols and symbolic gestures that can vivify and vitalize the words and texts of rites. Because there is still something there, some power there, even in those shrunken, shriveled, dried up forms: bread as wafer, the breaking of the bread as a crisp and tidy crackle, the baptismal bath as a trickle of water across the head, the sprinkling as some drops that few can see or feel, the oil as a quick smudge to be wiped off at once, the laying on of hands as a pat on the head, the incense as an invisible and unsmellable few grains on a quarter piece of charcoal, and so on and so on and so on.

But there is still something there. What is alarming and crippling is that now, when we can open up the symbols again, when we can make the eucharistic bread real bread that can be broken and shared, when immersion in baptism is again an option, we are not universally doing these things. Even young clergy who should know better are, more often than not, busy eliminating much of our symbol and body language in favor of more chatter, endless and infuriating pedagogy or commentary. Even if their words were carefully and poetically prepared it would be much too much, but when the monologues are idle and impromptu they cry to heaven for vengeance.

The presider who is trying to serve the people well will cultivate the practice of corporate silence in liturgical services at appropriate times—e.g., after the invitation to the opening prayer and before the collect; after readings, especially when there is no sung responsory; after homily, especially when there is no dialogue; after the vocal intercessions for those too bashful to pray aloud; after communion.

An inadequate period of silence, however, leaves an impression that is uncomfortable and coldly rubrical. One can sense the impatience and anxiety in a presider who simply has to get on with the words, who cannot allow the silence to become real for the congregation. Silence in a corporate sense takes some time to establish itself. Silence does not begin until the coughing and the shuffling stop. Appreciation of silence is felt by the assembly more slowly still. If one can discipline oneself to allow three minutes or more of silence after communion, for example, it can become one of the richest parts of the eucharistic rite for most of those present.

There are also other opportunities for silence. Using silence instead of customary words to accompany a liturgical action or gesture, like the sign of the cross, can enhance both the gesture and other spoken words. Just occasionally it would not hurt and it might refresh to forgo the vocalization and let the action stand on its own two (sturdy—sturdier than we give them credit for) feet. The few experimental efforts at nonverbal rites of common prayer of which this author has heard have been reported, without exception, as quite remarkable experiences by those present.

Only a few experiences of this sort—or even theatre experiences of mime or dance—could suffice to open up persons who regularly preside in liturgy to the immense impact of gesture, body language, visuals and other sensory elements in liturgical celebration.

Formerly it was customary, at least in some traditions, to warn presiders or presiders-to-be about what was called "the custody of the eyes." It seems to have been a part of the "sacred alias" atmosphere. The eyes were supposed to be downcast or fixed to the ceiling's tracery. Now that our sisters and brothers are coming back as primary signs of the Lord's presence, presiders are encouraged to look at them. And congregations are encour-

The uses of corporate silence

The eyes of the presider

75

aged, in places that are active, to overcome their fascination with print and with "following along" so that they can lift their heads and look at one another and at their ministers.

Although the tracery and the floor (and books or leaflets in the hands of the congregation) still have their devotees, they are a breed that will vanish as liturgical renewal progresses. Ministers increasingly recognize that, while they should not and need not devour the congregation with their eyes, there should be a constant exchange of interested, compassionate, encouraging looks not only during the readings and the homily, but also during prayers and songs and silences.

For those who can see, attention with the eyes is a simple and elementary sine qua non of corporate action and participation. Good celebration requires that kind of attention. Those interested, compassionate, encouraging looks have to be mutual. It doesn't do any good for the presider to look at the congregation, if the congregation's heads are buried in books or missalettes. The congregation certainly may use printed or visual materials for song and for unfamiliar responses, just as the presider may use a bible or lectionary and a sacramentary or other service book, but for neither should this mean eyes glued to book and a total loss of eye contact with others.

Custody of the tongue

Now our problem in many places is custody of the tongue. The pastoral responsibility of adaptations and increasing liturgical options, along with the recovered sense of need for hospitality and dialogue and participation, has occasioned (not caused) a certain immodesty in some presiders. The liturgical reforms were intended to make us more careful of the words we use. But the immodesty one notices is characterized by carelessness.

Perhaps some presiders are simply nervous about their new responsibilities. Perhaps there is not yet enough consciousness of and attention to the spirit of awe and reverence discussed earlier in these pages. But the fact is that some presiders talk entirely too much. Some apparently feel called upon by spirits (who shall be unnamed) to offer a running commentary which covers the ritual action like a heavy and almost impenetrable syrup. The clear but no doubt unintended implication is that the rite itself is hopelessly obscure and without any capacity to signify.

The opposite is more likely to be true. The rites have structure, movement, alternations, as well as gestures, symbols, texts that can and will signify if they are allowed to live and breathe. Good presiders will give the rites that freedom, will adapt with care and use words sparingly—and with the quality of imagery and poetry. They will facilitate the rite—i.e., the congregation's use of the rite. They will not crush from it all life and breath by either heavyhanded "instruction" or breezy and idle chatter.

If the presider is sufficiently disciplined to prepare very carefully any words that will be used in liturgical celebration, the possibility of falling into this verbosity trap will be almost eliminated. And if the presider can add to that discipline a sense of human limits and a modesty about one's small clerical contribution to a large ecclesial action, then the clerical tongue can become a friend rather than an enemy of liturgy.

Several years ago, in a colloquium on the human person and symbol at St. John's Abbey, Collegeville, Minnesota, a philosopher named Alphonso Lingis, then at Penn State, spoke about the symbolic function of persons and things. Rehearsing just a skeletal outline of what he said might be more helpful here than a smile school. Our point is not to suggest facial expressions appropriate to public rites, but rather to encourage presiders to feel the significance of face and hands in communications with others.

Speaking of symbolic function, Lingis said that what is given is not identical with being, because what is given is access to something beyond. One does not comprehend the symbol, because the symbol introduces one to what is beyond. When a face faces, it is like the surface any sensible object has—a new kind of distance is opened. To address oneself to the face of another is to face the other, the stranger. Conversation plays across this distance. We strive to reduce the other's alien character. But the other remains other, with the power to contest one's interpretation of things. The other can always withdraw. There is a dimension of alterity, a dimension of absence that the face presents to one.

The other faces you and speaks, with voice, gesture, hands for exploring, touching, feeling. The movements of the hands belong

The face and "alterity"

to the full order of the face. To face someone is to be exposed to that person. One comes with the poverty and nakedness of the face. You are the rich one, who has something to say, something to offer. You discover your life is a source and resource. To answer another is to expose yourself to the other's judgment. The other always requires something of you. You must answer in your own name, and in answering discover the singularity of your own existence. There is poverty and nakedness in the face of the other, but the other also rises before you in majesty and power. There is a symbolic function in the very structure of the face. The face presented is there to present the presence of absence. Absence commands the whole order of symbolization. Western thought has defined things too much in terms of bare presence, limiting being by neglecting the dimension of absence.

That brief outline of some of Lingis's remarks is for reflection and meditation. They are fragments, sentences out of a long paper, fallibly transcribed. This author has reread them periodically for several years and shares them here, risking an injustice to Lingis, out of a conviction that presiders need to feel some of this about their own faces and about the faces of the rest of the assembly, about their own hands and the hands of the rest of the assembly. Just to be aware of this quality of mystery, absence, hiddenness in face and hands is to give the edge to spirit in any possible conflict with presiding techniques.

On a more prosaic level, the reflection in facial expression of presence and attention to and involvement in what is going on in every moment of liturgical celebration is something the assembly needs. One's face reflects preoccupations, anxieties, withdrawals, distances, any of which is extremely damaging to the assembly's sense of unity and purpose.

Some people smile a lot. Others do not. These natural predispositions seem much less important to presiding style than being natural, and not feigning a temperament one does not possess. To be appreciative of people and their liturgical deed, to be oneself, to be reverent and to be collected—these are the great gifts the face bestows on a liturgical assembly.

**Hands across
the border**

It is no accident that the language of human love is so much a language of the hands, nor that persons who are without speech or hearing communicate with a sign language of the hands. Anyone can easily observe the difference between a speaker or even a conversationalist whose hands are a natural part of the communication and one whose passions, body, hands seem absent from the content of the remarks.

So it is not surprising that the liturgies of Christians made so much of the hands. The sharing of the Spirit in traditional sacramental language is the laying on of hands. The same gesture communicates the presence of the church, the mutuality of the sharing of charisms among the members of the church and between the faith community, through its designated representatives, and its individual members. The laying on of hands, as Godfrey Diekmann, O.S.B. has shown, is one of the most fundamental and universal of all sacramental gestures. Even in the portayal of the eucharistic prayer, some ancient iconography shows the hands of the presider placed upon the gifts rather than in the orante (outstretched) position.

It is obvious that personal habits and temperaments are relevant to the helpful and illustrative use of the hands in speech, but this fact should not deter presiders who are by nature more constricted and more rigid from endeavoring to loosen up themselves, their bodies, and, especially, their hands. Body and hands go together with the self, so an improvement in any area will be an improvement in all, whether through group work that makes one more at ease with people and in leading people, or through exposure to the theatre arts, or through a program of physical exercise to promote grace and coordination and the full and free use of the body.

It is not only in broad, full gestures that the presider communicates significantly with the hands, but also in handling the symbols and other objects which are an essential part of liturgical celebration. Everything that is used in liturgy should be handled in a way, a manner that speaks to the assembly without words. Not only should the presider's reverence for the assembly itself be palpable, but also the presider's reverence and respect for the liturgical book, the scriptures, the water, the oil, the bread and wine, altar, cross, vessels, sprinkler, censer, whatever.

The assembly cannot benefit a great deal from a presider's interior reverence for the people, if outwardly the presider treats the people like a herd of sheep. The herd psychology is what will be felt, because that is what is observed. It drowns out any other vibrations. Nor does it help the assembly much if a presider has an interior feeling for the symbols and objects dealt with in celebration, but to all appearances is embarrassed by them, ashamed to hold them up and out so that they can be seen and otherwise sensed, inclined to employ them in a furtive and half-concealed way. Seeing is believing.

The hands of the presider, then, must open not only themselves and the presider's being to the assembly, not only the words spoken and prayed, but also everything that they handle in the course of a rite. The hands express care for the symbol or other object. The hands express the commonality of the thing—the fact that it is not the presider's private property but the possession of the whole assembly. The hands express praise and thanksgiving for the thing, holding it up before the assembly so that all can experience its use and praise the Lord for its beauty. The hands can do all this, once they are appreciated and limbered up and choreographed (in a manner of speaking) like all the rest of the assembly's liturgical action.

The hands of the presider will be this kind of communicator and will do these things more appropriately if they are naked, plain and unadorned—i.e., without rings, wrist watches, bracelets, or other distracting superfluities. There are liturgical garments (see below) suitable for these occasions, but ordinary jewelry does not qualify. If an episcopal ring is considered to belong to the liturgical garment category, it could be an exception.

It's not heavy, it's my druthers

We should think, too, about our posture, carriage and bearing, while we are considering the body's brilliance and effectiveness in communicating. The visual and experiential impact of one's posture and carriage is influential even when people are not conscious of it.

In days not too long past, a caricature of the presiding clergyperson might have shown a figure with shoulders bowed, as if carrying an extremely heavy weight, head laid wearily on the right shoulder or the left, eyes on the ground, hands clasped tightly before the belly, struggling along against a felt but imaginary headwind. The message was clear and the Care packages arrived with satisfying regularity. Behind such an image lay a pile of problems that could not be resolved until a thoroughgoing ecclesial reform (like the one whose initial stages we are experiencing) was undertaken.

Those whose function it was to preside paid a great price for those Care packages. Whether the presider was frail and small or big and burly, that image evoked pity. Poor dear, poor, poor dear, who had given up so much, who was victim of a long, lone struggle against the world, the flesh and the devil. *Everything* was on his shoulders . . . and he looked it.

Now, however, the presider must be asked to look as if the job is not a crushing burden or a bore but a freely chosen service and servanthood in a community of shared faith, shared prayer, shared mission, shared responsibility. Everything is no longer on the presider's shoulders. The church's witness, the church's worship, the church's service to the world—all of these now rest on the shoulders of all the baptized, as they should. That is where they belong.

So the presider has been liberated and should look it! The presider should look like a person who has willingly accepted the delegation of the community for this particular ministerial task. A free person in Christ Jesus, the presider can stand straight and confident, but with a reverence and awe befitting the assembly's God-centeredness and totally unlike human self assertion or bravado.

That conscious and constant attention to posture and bearing on the part of the presider will elicit a comparable attention and alertness among the other ministers and the members of the congregation. Carelessness and slouchiness beget the same, but if the visual frame which the presider occupies shows something else, something more appealing, more aware, more noble and elevating, the whole assembly will be the better for it.

Careful planning and preparation will assure that the movements of the presider during a rite will be certain and purposeful. Like carriage, these movements are framed visually by the congregation. They speak to the congregation a message that can help or hurt the celebration. If they speak of hurry and haste, they induce a certain panic or restlessness. If they convey indecision and forgetfulness, they are a bore and a burden. If they indicate a need-

**Movement
without haste**

less scurrying about for materials that should have been placed properly before the rite began, they mutely invite the congregation to a similar lack of care.

But if the presider's movements during the celebration are never needless, always direct and deliberate and without haste, apparently at ease in the environment and with the furniture and with all the other people, then the grace of the scene will not be lost on anyone. For a prod in the right direction, remember Chevy Chase on NBC's "Saturday Night." Anyone who has been around for a while has witnessed episodes almost as chaotic in ritual action.

To repeat a suggestion, one thing that can help the entire congregation, especially persons with specific ministerial functions, become more aware of the body's communicative power in public assemblies is the occasional employment of dance or mime artists or actors in liturgical celebrations. It is something that is *caught,* from the experience of others who know how to handle their bodies and use them maximally, rather than taught with the concepts and words we have to deal with in a manual of this sort.

Dressing up for an occasion

Liturgical vesture is a question totally different from the question of clerical garb in daily life. Those countries and cultures in which clergy ordinarily wear a distinctive garb most of the time may well be reviewing the extent to which this custom relates to some of the clerical problems discussed above. Although the subject is tempting, comments on the appropriateness or inappropriateness of clerical garb in ordinary life are beyond the scope of this liturgical treatise. Like the distinctive daily dress of some clergy, the robes worn by some ecclesiastical dignitaries at civil and other non-liturgical public occasions are in no way related to liturgical vesture.

The vesture of the presider in liturgical celebrations (and, by implication, that of other specifically functioning ministers), however, is very much within this book's scope. Liturgical vestments have to do with the celebration itself, its total environment, and the function of the presider in a particular role of service in the liturgical assembly.

In her book accompanying an exhibition of The Art Institute of Chicago, *Raiment for the Lord's Service—A Thousand Years of Western Vestments,* Christa C. Mayer-Thurman notes that "vestments have gone the full cycle, from very simple, generously cut robes, made of silk, linen, or wool, to the rich, elaborate but most distracting achievements of later centuries, to contemporary re-introduction of early Christian simplicity in purpose, form and function" (The Art Institute of Chicago, 1975, p. 11).

Horace T. Allen, Jr. also contributed to the volume and speaks of shifting "the significance and functioning of these sacramentals [vestments] from their reference to the wearer to the definition of corporate occasion. . . . His or her garments are 'sacred,' therefore, not by association with himself or herself, but with his or her function within the community and the garments' functioning for the whole community" (p. 23).

This approach seems sound and helps to deal with problems some contemporary clergy obviously are feeling. Those who recognize the distance that a great many forces and practices have created between congregations and their clergy may be tempted at times to think that the elimination of the chasuble might help close the gap. There are a lot of things to be done to close the gap, but depriving the liturgical assembly and the ritual action of this focus of color, form and design is hardly one of them.

Beauty, sober dignity, fullness rather than skimpiness, a flowing rather than a restricted (cinctured) wearing, celebrative color and appropriately abstract (for a garment) ornamentation—these are qualities that spring to mind when one begins to think of vesture as a part of one's service to the community and its liturgical deed.

"It is certain," Aidan Kavanagh, O.S.B. writes in the same book, "that cultures have and will interpret these determinants and their modes of execution in various media differently. But the norms to which the nature of the liturgical act and its presuppositions give rise are broad enough to allow for this variety of interpretation. Yet even the broadest of norms still has limits. Vestments that are trivial by the standards of the culture that uses them, or vestments that are serious according to norms other than those to which the act of worship itself gives rise, not only transgress the authentic sentiment of the community but comment on a shift of Christian sentiment into areas foreign to the basic purposes of Christian worship—areas such as aestheticism, triumphalism, saccharine emotionalism, or cheap tastelessness.

The liturgical garment then becomes less than sacred, a mere vehicle for applied 'symbolism' chosen at whim; less than a garment, a mere costume overly ornamented and ignoble in form; a billboard whose purpose is to shout ideologies instead of clothing a creature in beauty" (p. 15).

When the congregation and other ministers look at a presider during a celebration of common prayer, the critically important realization is that the presider is their own, one with them, identified with them, loving them and serving them. When that realization is alive and operative, then the distinctive liturgical vesture which contributes focus, color, form and beauty to the action is theirs too. When that realization is absent, however, no raiment or lack of raiment will make any difference.

"It is a body-thing . . ."

One way to signify, and therefore reinforce, such a realization (as well as the realization of a number of other basic principles with which this manual has concerned itself) is a very simple gesture at the beginning and, perhaps also, at the end of a liturgical celebration. Part of this author's memory of seminary days at St. John's Abbey in Collegeville, Minnesota is an indelibly etched picture of the monks entering choir. Two by two, they reverenced the altar and then turned and reverenced each other with a bow before they went to their seats.

If we really see the congregation and its presider as primary signs of the presence of Jesus Christ, a simple gesture might do more for our ecclesiology and for our liturgy than a monograph on the subject. After the ministers, including the presider, bow to the altar at the beginning of a celebration, let them turn and bow with reverence also toward the congregation. Or, more fully perhaps, let them turn and bow with reverence toward each distinguishable (by seating) sector of the congregation. The congregation, in turn, bows back. As with all gestures, the point is not to talk about it but to do it. The congregation will be shy at first, will slowly respond, and will grow to appreciate it.

Writing in the January 1972 issue of *Liturgy,* The Liturgical Conference membership journal, Eugene Walsh, S.S. said a definitive word about style: "Worship is a human experience, not a set of concepts. It is a thing of beauty and warmth. It is a body-thing, not a head-thing. There is no way for one to think oneself into being a good presider. One has got to get it into one's muscles and bones, just like dancers, actors and ballplayers."

What Geoffrey Wood wrote on the theme ("The Bishop") of the November 1976 issue of *Liturgy* applies in a real sense to all who preside in public worship: "Bishops take on the role of leadership. They are obliged to bring us home, guide us to the truth, to a communion of saints. Then they must not simply indulge in the rhetoric of love. They must take the mask off our 'independence,' reveal our relatedness with vigor, evoke our physical and spiritual need for each other, declare it 'legitimate'— this seemingly negative thing, our need for each other, which if allowed to come out could flood the world with warmth and care . . .

"To do this effectively bishops and priests must get in touch with their own personal need for relatedness. They must risk feeling it and expressing it. That's all. The moment they do, they will be loved; they will move us. Abyss calls to abyss. Actually we don't have to be led anywhere but to each other. Then the kingdom appears."

Resources

Blessed and Broken: An Exploration of the Contemporary Experience of God in Eucharistic Celebration. Ralph A. Kiefer. Wilmington, Del.: Michael Glazier, 1982.

The Body at Liturgy. Joe Wise. Cincinnati: North American Liturgy Resources, 1975.

Documents on the Liturgy, 1963–1979, Conciliar, Papal, and Curial Texts. International Committee on English in the Liturgy, Inc. Collegeville, Minn.: The Liturgical Press, 1983.

Elements of Rite: A Handbook of Liturgical Style. Aidan Kavanagh. New York: Pueblo Publishing Co., 1982.

Everybody Steals from God: Communication as Worship. Eugene Fischer. Notre Dame, Ind.: University of Notre Dame Press, 1977.

The Leadership of Worship. H. G. Hardin. Nashville: Abingdon Press, 1980.

Liturgy (Quarterly). Washington: The Liturgical Conference. Subscription periodical.

Liturgy Made Simple. Mark Searle. Collegeville, Minn.: The Liturgical Press, 1981.

Liturgy Committee Handbook. Virginia Sloyan, ed. Washington: The Liturgical Conference, 1971.

Liturgy with Style and Grace. Gabe Huck. Chicago: Liturgy Training Program, 1978.

The Meaning of Ritual. Leonel Mitchell. New York: Paulist Press, 1977.

The Ministry of the Celebrating Community. Eugene A. Walsh. Glendale, Ariz.: Pastoral Arts Associates, 1979.

New Liturgy, New Laws. R. Kevin Seasoltz. Collegeville, Minn.: The Liturgical Press, 1980.

Parish: A Place for Worship. Mark Searle, ed. Collegeville, Minn., The Liturgical Press, 1981.

The Pastor as Worship Leader. Frank Senn. Minneapolis: Augsburg Publishing House, 1977.

Persons in Liturgical Celebrations. Lucien Deiss. Chicago: World Library, 1978.

Practical Suggestions for Celebrating Sunday Mass. Eugene A. Walsh. Glendale, Ariz.: Pastoral Arts Associates, 1978.

The Prayer Tradition of Black People. Harold A. Carter. Valley Forge, Penn.: Judson Press, 1976.

Real Presence: Worship, Sacraments, and Commitment. Regis A. Duffy. San Francisco: Harper and Row, 1982.

The Shape of Baptism: The Rite of Christian Initiation. Aidan Kavanagh. New York: Pueblo Publishing Co., 1978.

Signs, Words, and Gestures: Short Homilies on the Liturgy. Balthasar Fischer. New York: Pueblo Publishing Co., 1981.

Soulfull Worship. Clarence J. Rivers. Washington: The National Office for Black Catholics, 1974.

Spirit and Song of the New Liturgy. Lucien Deiss. Cincinnati: World Library, 1970.

The Study of Liturgy. Cheslyn Jones, Geoffrey Wainwright, and Edward Yarnold. New York: Oxford University Press, 1978.

Sunday Morning: A Time for Worship. Mark Searle, ed. Collegeville, Minn.: The Liturgical Press, 1982.

A Theology of Celebration. Eugene A. Walsh. Glendale, Ariz.: Pastoral Arts Associates, 1979.

To Give Thanks and Praise: General Instruction of the Roman Missal with Commentary for Musicians and Priests. Ralph A. Kiefer. Washington: National Association of Pastoral Musicians, 1980.

Touchstones for Liturgical Ministers. Virginia Sloyan, ed. Washington: The Liturgical Conference, 1978.

Worship (Bimonthly). Collegeville, Minn.: The Liturgical Press. Subscription periodical.

List prepared by Mary Frohlich.